**Routledge Performance Practitioners** is a series of introductory guides to the key theatre-makers of the last century. Each volume explains the background to and the work of one of the major influences on twentieth- and twenty-first-century performance.

These compact, well-illustrated and clearly written books will unravel the contribution of modern theatre's most charismatic innovators. *Eugenio Barba* is the first book to combine:

- an overview of Barba's work and that of his company, Odin Teatret
- exploration of his writings and ideas on theatre anthropology, and his unique contribution to contemporary performance research
- in-depth analysis of the 2000 production of *Ego Faust*, performed at the International School of Theatre Anthropology
- a practical guide to training exercises developed by Barba and the actors in the company.

As a first step towards critical understanding, and as an initial exploration before going on to further, primary research, **Routledge Performance Practitioners** are unbeatable value for today's student.

**Jane Turner** is Principal Lecturer in the Department of Contemporary Arts and the programme leader for BA (Hons) in Contemporary Theatre and Performance ... ...y.

# ROUTLEDGE PERFORMANCE PRACTITIONERS

Series editor: Franc Chamberlain, University College Northampton

Routledge Performance Practitioners is an innovative series of introductory handbooks on key figures in twentieth-century performance practice. Each volume focuses on a theatre-maker whose practical and theoretical work has in some way transformed the way we understand theatre and performance. The books are carefully structured to enable the reader to gain a good grasp of the fundamental elements underpinning each practitioner's work. They will provide an inspiring springboard for future study, unpacking and explaining what can initially seem daunting.

The main sections of each book cover:

* personal biography
* explanation of key writings
* description of significant productions
* reproduction of practical exercises.

Volumes currently available in the series are:

*Eugenio Barba* by Jane Turner
*Augusto Boal* by Frances Babbage
*Michael Chekhov* by Franc Chamberlain
*Anna Halprin* by Libby Worth and Helen Poynor
*Jacques Lecoq* by Simon Murray
*Vsevolod Meyerhold* by Jonathan Pitches
*Konstantin Stanislavsky* by Bella Merlin

Future volumes will include:

*Pina Bausch*
*Bertolt Brecht*
*Peter Brook*
*Etienne Decroux*
*Jerzy Grotowski*
*Joan Littlewood*
*Ariane Mnouchkine*
*Lee Strasberg*
*Robert Wilson*

# EUGENIO
# BARBA

*Jane Turner*

**Routledge**
Taylor & Francis Group

LONDON AND NEW YORK

First published 2004
by Routledge
2 Park Square, Milton Park, Abingdon, Oxon OX14 4RN

Simultaneously published in the USA and Canada
by Routledge
270 Madison Ave, New York, NY 10016

*Routledge is an imprint of the Taylor & Francis Group*

© 2004 Jane Turner

Typeset in Perpetua by
Florence Production Ltd, Stoodleigh, Devon
Printed and bound in Great Britain by
TJ International Ltd, Padstow, Cornwall

*British Library Cataloguing in Publication Data*
A catalogue record for this book is available from
the British Library

*Library of Congress Cataloging in Publication Data*
    Turner, Jane, 1960 Nov. 21–
    Eugenio Barba/Jane Turner.
       p. cm. – (Routledge performance practitioners)
    Includes bibliographical references and index.
    1. Barba, Eugenio – Criticism and interpretation.   2. Odin Teatret.
    I. Title.   II. Series.
    PN2688.B33T87 2004
    792.02′33′092–dc22                                        2004004779

ISBN 0-415-27327-7 (hbk)
ISBN 0-415-27328-5 (pbk)

# CONTENTS

# FIGURES

# ACKNOWLEDGEMENTS

I am greatly indebted to all at Odin Teatret and would like to thank them all, especially Eugenio Barba, for their generous support, time and cooperation. I would also like to thank Annelis Kuhlmann and Rina Skeel for their help during Odin Week 2003. Special thanks go to Martin Blain and Bev Stevens for their help and encouragement throughout this project. Thank you to Patrice Pavis for so generously sending me the text of his 'Intercultural Analysis' article. Thank you also to Jan Rüsz, Tony D'Urso and Fiora Bemporad for their very fine photographs housed in the Odin Teatret archive and reproduced here in this book. Thank you also to colleagues at MMU Cheshire and CTP students. Finally, I would like to thank Franc Chamberlain for all his help, advice and support.

# BUILDING A
# 'SMALL TRADITION'

Eugenio Barba is a theatre director, an actor trainer and a writer (see Figure 1.1). With his actors in the Odin Teatret, Barba has developed a distinct approach to actor training and making theatre performances. He has written detailed books, essays and papers on his work and many other aspects of theatre. As well as being a co-founder of Odin Teatret, he is also a founder of the International School of Theatre Anthropology (**ISTA**), where the craft of the actor is examined and explored. A large amount of his work with Odin Teatret and ISTA has been documented both in writing and on video. Therefore, it is important to note that this book sits within a web of writings and other documentary materials that you might be interested in consulting to gain a fuller understanding of Barba's work and ideas. In partnership with the writings and video material, it is essential also to have a practical understanding of Barba's theatre work. Throughout this book, and especially in Chapter 4, you will be given exercises to try that will give you a practical sense of Barba's particular approach to the craft of the actor.

A key experience that informed Barba's attitude in both life and theatre comes from his leaving Italy as a teenager and going to Norway. In Norway he had a variety of menial jobs and first discovered and experienced two aspects of human behaviour that were to have a profound influence on him. While in Norway he experienced both

**Figure 1.1** Eugenio Barba, ISTA, 2000. Photograph by Fiora Bemporad

generosity and rejection because he was a foreigner. These two experiences created what he now calls 'two wounds', and they have influenced
the way in which he has gone on to make theatre. Although there is no
'common philosophy' in his work that Barba would acknowledge, he
says that the 'two wounds' have constituted Odin Teatret's professional
identity.

## THE BEGINNING OF THE JOURNEY

Eugenio Barba was born in southern Italy in October 1936. His father
was an officer in the Italian army, who died from an illness when Barba
was ten years of age. At 14, in 1951, Barba was sent to military college
to follow in his father's footsteps and train for a career in the army
but the regime was repressive and Barba rebelled against it. More
significantly, this was also the year that he recalls first going to the
theatre. The production was of *Cyrano De Bergerac* and the most notable
aspect of the production for Barba was the presence of a live horse on
the stage. In comparison with the horse the actors' gestures were like

pantomime and their characters were crude caricatures. The actors merely pretended to laugh, cry, be surprised or out of breath; they lacked energy and conviction. The horse was not acting. The horse was not pretending to be something else but was playing an important role. The actions of the horse were not imitation or affected like in pantomime but were what Barba considered 'real' actions. As a consequence, the **energy** or **presence** exuded by the horse was what continually attracted Barba's attention, not the acting by the human beings. Although it was not innovatory to have live animals onstage, there was a quality in the literal presence of the horse that excited Barba and led him to embark on his theatrical journey. His intention has been to create theatre where the presence and actions of the actors can be as exciting as those he identified in the horse and these ideas have continued to intrigue him and have informed his research into the presence of the actor on the stage.

Three years later in 1954, when Barba finally graduated from military college, he chose to travel to Norway. In Norway he took a job as a welder, then as a sailor in the merchant navy on the freighter *Talabot*, which enabled him to travel to many parts of the world, most notably to India (later in his career *Talabot* was used as the title of an Odin performance). At 20 he enrolled at the University of Oslo and gained a degree in Norwegian, French and the History of Religion. It was at this point that Barba determined to embark on a theatrical journey. In the video documentary *A Way Through Theatre*, Barba explains, perhaps a little sardonically, that his choice of a career in theatre at this time was so that his temperamental behaviour could be explained as artistic temperament and, therefore, interesting rather than difficult. With the aid of a scholarship from **UNESCO**, Barba spent a year studying directing at a theatre school in Warsaw, Poland. He notes that it was seeing a film by the Polish film director Andrzej Wajda titled *Ashes and Diamonds* that inspired him to go to Poland (again, as with the title *Talabot*, it can be noted how this particular film that so influenced his life was later used by Barba as the title of his book about his years in Poland).

## IN SEARCH OF A LOST THEATRE

Poland at this time was staunchly **socialist** and strictly patrolled by a censorious police regime but it had a cultural policy that supported artistic practices, including theatre. Barba took every opportunity to see theatre, travel the country and to meet and talk with actors, directors and writers. On several occasions he met with a young Polish director named Jerzy **Grotowski**. Their long, hard talking about life, politics and theatre led Grotowski to invite Barba to come and be his assistant at the Theatre of Thirteen Rows in Opole. Barba had begun to feel depressed and suffocated by Poland but the meetings with Grotowski and the bond of friendship that had begun to develop between them led Barba to accept the invitation. He announced to his tutor at the university that he intended leaving and completing his work for the diploma in directing at the Theatre of Thirteen Rows. The oppressiveness of the society at the time makes the work that emerged from theatres, especially from the tiny theatre in Opole, even more remarkable. Barba suggests that a part of what drew him and Grotowski together was a shared 'fight against adverse circumstances, indifference and solitude, with the need to invent a home – a theatre – for themselves on their own terms' (Barba, 1999a: 11). For the next three years Barba observed and learnt his theatrical craft from Grotowski. Although he did not complete the work for the diploma, he wrote and published articles about Grotowski's work that gained the work an international audience. He is noted as being the associate director on Grotowski's production *Akropolis*, now considered to be one of the most important theatre productions of the twentieth century. *In Search of a Lost Theatre* (1965) was written by Barba and published in Italy and is the first book written about Grotowski's work. Later, other early articles were collated and edited by Barba under the title *Towards a Poor Theatre* (see Grotowski, 1969), generally regarded to be one of the most important books written about theatre.

Barba notes that Grotowski's theatre productions were limited by the demands of the censors working for the socialist regime. As long as a theatre production was based on a literary text that the censors considered acceptable, they would allow the work to go ahead. For example, Wyspianski's play *Akropolis* was acceptable to the censors and so, although Grotowski was intending to do a version of the play set in a concentration camp, he was given permission to perform it. For both Grotowski and Barba this was a time when they learnt to fight against 'adverse circumstances' and began to build a theatre 'on their own terms'.

The formalisation of the acting style that Grotowski's actors worked with attracted Barba because here was something that could compete with the live horse that he had seen on the stage in *Cyrano De Bergerac*. Barba learnt from Grotowski what it is to create a tradition and how an actor might then go on to embody and transform that tradition, that is, train so the body understands the approach to performing and then make the approach her or his own. The same exercises can be used for different purposes and for different individual needs. For example, Barba used the same exercises that Grotowski used with his actors but for different reasons. We can see from the video on *Physical Training at the Odin Teatret* (1972) that some of the exercises are similar to those described in *Towards a Poor Theatre*. Exercises, Barba says, are like bricks that can be used to build whatever we want; they serve the context in which we work.

In addition to the exercises in Chapter 4, there are exercises that punctuate both this chapter and Chapter 2. You are invited to try these exercises as they offer you an alternative way of understanding the work that Barba has developed with his actors. The exercises in Chapter 4 are derived from Barba's and the Odin actors' work and, having tried them, you can then transform them to your own individual context to make them work for your own individual needs. The important point is that, whatever the method of training or performing that an actor chooses to explore, it must always be embodied, that is the actor needs to take the approach and make it his or her own, both physically and mentally.

The experience of working with Grotowski made a distinct impression on Barba. It showed him that the theatre he sought to make would be a struggle against the dominant ideas of the time and that he would need to build his own space of 'freedom and difference'. He also learnt from Grotowski that a theatre group should never give up on, or be deterred from, what it believes and that theatre's function is essential to the health and well being of society. This often means that theatre asks difficult questions about the way people live their lives and the rules that are imposed by people on other people. Grotowski lived in Poland at a time when people did not tell others what they could and should do; the people who represented the political regime did that. As a consequence, Barba states that neither he nor Grotowski became didactic teachers like the Russian theatre practitioner Konstantin **Stanislavsky**, who, as well as directing, developed his approach to the training of actors in Russia at the turn of the twentieth century. Vsevolod **Meyerhold**, who was also an actor trainer and director and worked in Russia, developed a less didactic approach with his actors, arguably because he was working under a more repressive political regime than Stanislavsky.

As well as theatre needing to work with the ideas of 'freedom and difference', Barba says we all need to find our own 'moment of truth'. By this he means that each of us needs to build our own 'home', our own theatre, and find our own way to act and make theatre, although, he adds, we can always use the advice from those we encounter on our journey, who have already built their own 'home'.

Before Barba returned to Norway, he again travelled to India, where he was introduced to the training and performance practices of **Kathakali**. After six months travelling in India, Barba was able to return for a short time to Poland, despite his visa having expired. However, the authorities then refused to renew the visa and Barba was forced to return to Norway to find work in the theatre there. His intention was to work as a director in the traditional theatre, but not being a native speaker of Norwegian, Barba was not considered a suitable candidate. As theatre in Norway at that time was very traditional, subsidised and commercial, Barba determined to set up his own company based on the principles that he had learnt from Grotowski and the Kathakali tradition.

## BUILDING HIS OWN 'HOME'

In 1964 Barba, at the age of 27, founded the Odin Teatret in Oslo. The name Odin comes from the name given to the Norse god of war. The story of the god Odin depicts a god who, in addition to representing war, is also considered to be the god of 'light through darkness' and a god of wisdom. According to the Norse myth, his wisdom is derived from having travelled towards death and darkness but by cutting himself free and being filled with light he was able to return to life. Thus it is that he understands how to transform the destructive elements of the darkness into light (see Taviani in Barba, 1986a: 237).

From the founding of Odin Teatret, Barba's work and that of the Odin Teatret are almost inseparable. Although this is a book about the theatre work of Eugenio Barba, from this point on Odin and the Odin actors will be substantially referred to and should be read as including Barba, unless otherwise stated.

The original theatre company of 11 or so were gathered from aspiring actors who had all failed to get a place at the Oslo Theatre School. They all had jobs of work during the day and so were only able to train at night. Quickly their number dwindled to five and then to four. The training was arduous and for many of the would-be actors it appeared to be pointless, as they were not rehearsing for a perform-ance. Barba would not compromise his work: he believed that the actors should aim 'to live as an actor without living for performance' (Taviani in Barba, 1986a: 246). Using exercises, experimenting with theatrical forms that were only partially understood, and training for the sake of training, were all ideas virtually unheard of in Europe in the early 1960s. However, the conventional theatre of Scandinavia was soon to become far more diverse and inclusive of such unusual approaches to theatre. Of the four original actors who first joined Odin Teatret in Norway, Else Marie Lauvik and Torgeir Wethal remain in the company to this day.

*Ornitofilene* was the company's first performance, performed 50 times from October 1965. As with the other productions that Odin has subsequently created, the performance was improvised through rehearsal. Unlike many of their later performances, *Ornitofilene* fol-lowed Grotowski's approach of working from a literary text that the company transformed into a dramatic text. This approach to making theatre was only used for the first three of their productions, although the idea of improvising did set the beginnings of their style and approach to making theatre that they still use today. One critic's comment, recorded in *The Floating Islands* (1979), describes the performance of *Ornitofilene* as 'a strange experience' which was impossible to talk about (Barba, 1979: 15).

## POLITICS AND RESISTING THE 'SPIRIT OF THE TIMES'

Although many of the young theatre companies in Europe and North America were making theatre that confronted the politics of their time, Odin resisted making overtly political work and, as a result, has often been considered to be apolitical. Barba and Odin may not have made theatre that was specifically opposed to the **Vietnam War**, for instance, but this is not to say that their work is, or was, not political. Their work has always reflected the deep concerns and issues that exist between human beings, questioning institutions and the implications of their governing of peoples' lives. But rather than making theatre located in a particular space about particular political or social issues, the company have chosen to work with myths and stories that transcend a particular time and place. Stories, myths, fables and folklore from all around the world have often been used as the bedrock of Odin's performances. One reason for this may be that from the earliest times people have told and listened to stories. As people travelled and found new homes, so stories also moved from place to place and this is very much like the experience that Barba and Odin have had. There are many shared histories and experiences mixed up in the stories that we tell and listen to, these stories are often not fixed in any one particular time or space but can be adapted and re-adapted to different times and spaces, and so stories have the potential to reach a very wide audience.

Working as an ensemble has meant that Odin has been able to resist the temptation to make work for other people, or work in a style that is fashionable. Odin's theatre work aims to fight what Barba calls the 'spirit of the times', that is, an agenda imposed by a political regime or ideology. Barba learnt early on that working as an ensemble gave the company strength; there could be shared aims, shared emotional ties, shared experiences and, most of all, a shared habitat.

Their work has often been described as being like a ritual but Barba has resisted this label, partly because in the 1960s this represented a trend. 'Ritual' became a fashionable label to give young and emerging theatre companies at the time. Spectators favoured theatre that accepted the label of ritual because it reflected the 'spirit of the time'. Barba suggests that this tells us more about the needs of the spectator than about the Odin Teatret work. Arguably, the description is not without validity as there are qualities in the work that may evoke a sense of ritual.

## A SIDE-STEP LOOK AT RITUAL

Ritual events often entail communication with another dimension, for example with a god or gods who are above the earth. Rituals can also confirm a sense of collective identity for a particular group and involve the participants in some sort of a transformation. The aim of the event is that it must be effective, or efficacious, in its intention whether that is making the gods happy, for instance, or driving sickness from a community, or transforming two people into a husband and wife.

A wedding is a ritual. When it takes place in a church, or other place of worship, a wedding would be considered sacred; however, a wedding can also be secular, that is, not religious. Whether it is sacred or secular, it gives those people involved a sense of a collective identity and transforms the two people named the bride and groom into husband and wife. Theatre can also be considered a ritual as it gives the spectators a collective sense of identity and both the space and the participants (or actors) are transformed for the duration of the event. Whereas sacred, or religious, ritual communicates on a vertical plane with a god or gods, theatrical ritual, like other secular rituals, is more earthbound and communicates on a horizontal plane. This might be understood simply as ritual entailing some form of belief from the participants whereas theatre entails the use of the participants' imagination. Theatre primarily aims to communicate to spectators and does not aim to be efficacious in the same way as ritual, although, as was stated earlier, theatre is important to the well being of individuals and society. Ritual, as a type of formalised behaviour, shares many common features with theatre and these commonalities have been studied and written about by academics and theatre practitioners, most notably, Victor **Turner** and Richard **Schechner**.

## THEATRE AS AN 'EMPTY RITUAL'

More recently Barba has said that he believes theatre to be an empty ritual, 'not because it is futile and senseless, but because it is not usurped by doctrine' (Watson *et al.*, 2002: 255). In the Odin Teatret's performance work the energy, actions and precision used in the re-enactment of a story, although divorced from a belief system, can be compared to the precision of actions used in rituals. Another similarity is the power of the performer's presence to conjure images and transport the spectator from their everyday existence to an **extra-daily** dimension. A particular performance that most notably demonstrates these similarities between ritual and Odin's performance work is *In the Skeleton of the Whale* (1997). The spectators, or witnesses, to this theatrical event are sat at long trestle tables down the two lengths of a studio space. The tables are covered with fine white linen cloths and have candles burning on them. Bowls of olives and bread, wine glasses and bottles of red wine are also set on the tables for the spectators. Other members of the company, often Barba himself, serve the wine to the spectators as the performers come into the space. The wine, food and candlelight create an atmosphere that, as spectators, we can connect with rituals and special events we have previously experienced. The event creates a very profound experience for many of the spectators of the performance: it is as if the performers are sharing something of themselves with us, a modern secular ritual perhaps. The performance creates a sense of what is called **communitas**, a collective experience, and it is the experience of the event that is important rather than what we think it might mean in concrete terms.

All theatre is performed in the here and now and, therefore, will always have connections with a time and space. Different associations will emerge for each spectator depending on the time and space in which the theatre piece is performed. As a spectator we do not always know the point of departure for the actor's performance: the logic or coherence of an Odin performance may not be immediately clear to us. But there are many moments that will resonate for a spectator, that might appear familiar, and we make our own associations with these moments and build our own **dramaturgy** for the performance. How and why the performances have such a profound impact on different spectators will be explored further in Chapter 3.

## ACTORS AS FLOATING ISLANDS

As with much of Barba's writing about theatre, the content of the performances resounds with many potential interpretations and readings. For example, in the title *In the Skeleton of the Whale* there is the figurative idea that the spectators, sitting down the sides of the space, are like the ribs of the whale. We, the collective audience, form the skeleton of the whale, which could be read figuratively as having consumed the Odin performances and performers. The spectators are presented with fragments from previous Odin productions that have been subtly woven into a new performance. A different reading is that the whale is a floating island that contains traces of all the performers, productions and spectators; the floating island is an image, or metaphor, used by Barba to describe the actor. His first book about the work at Odin was titled *The Floating Islands* (1979) and the second was titled *Beyond the Floating Islands* (1986a). One of the texts in *Beyond the Floating*

*Islands* is titled 'A Premise on Written Silence' and here he explains the use of the term in relation to his and the company's necessity to work as they do: 'the desire to remain foreign . . . the awareness that our action through theatre springs from an attitude towards existence that has its roots in one transnational and transcultural country' (Barba, 1986a: 10). This 'country' is envisaged by Barba as an archipelago, a group or chain of islands, of floating islands not rooted in any one place. We can see how the metaphor of the floating island has evolved from Barba's experience of being a foreigner in Norway and his aim that their work should not be rooted in the 'spirit of the time', that is, fixed in one time and place.

Working in Norway, without a space that was theirs and without any grant from the authorities, was very difficult to sustain despite the fact that their work was beginning to attract a following. They had toured *Ornitofilene* to other Scandinavian countries including Denmark. A nurse who lived in Holstebro, a northern town in Denmark, saw the performance. She, knowing that the city council were looking to implement a new cultural policy to develop and support the arts, talked to the mayor about the company and persuaded him to invite them to become the city's resident theatre company. A small grant of money was offered to them and an old farm was given to them as a base to work. Odin gratefully accepted the offer to move to Holstebro and slowly, over many years, have transformed the farm buildings into theatres and workshop-spaces, and put Holstebro firmly on the international theatre map.

On moving to Holstebro in 1966, Odin chose to define itself as an 'Inter-Scandinavian Theatre Laboratory for the Art of the Actor' (Barba, 1979: 15). This title was to ensure that people outside the company understood that they were not merely a theatre company that produced performances. Better known as Nordisk Teaterlaboratorium, or NTL, the organisation incorporated Odin Teatret and was concerned with providing a research space in Scandinavia for the study of theatre training and the actor in performance, both European and non-European, historic and contemporary.

## A 'SMALL TRADITION' AND NTL

The Odin Teatret has been resident in Holstebro for over 37 years. During this time the company have created what Barba calls a 'small tradition' that has become interwoven into theatrical genealogy: a theatrical family tree. All around the world there are theatre companies that make theatre work in a similar way to Odin; their ambition is to make the work that they believe is important and they have continued to work at their craft for many years, hence creating a 'small tradition'. One of the consequences of moving to Holstebro was that the work that the company produced had to resolve the problem of once again being considered foreign. The members of Odin Teatret itself were without a common culture or spoken language and Holstebro presented yet another cultural and linguistic obstacle for them to negotiate as none of the company spoke Danish. For this reason they had to build a different sort of dramaturgy, one that would interweave events, characters and song to make what Barba calls a 'theatre that dances'. Barba says theatre dances not only on the level of energy but also on the semantic level: 'It is its meaning that dances, sometimes explicitly, other times covertly' (Barba, 1990: 97). Having moved to Holstebro, the company recruited new members, including Iben Nagel Rasmussen, who is still performing with the company. The newly expanded company prepared their second production, titled *Kaspariana*, which was performed in 1967. (For detailed accounts of all the Odin Teatret performances, see Barba, 1979, 1999b; Christofferson, 1993; and Watson, 1993.)

The third production, *Ferai* (1969), was considered by audiences and critics to have been highly successful in Europe and Latin America but was stopped abruptly by Barba after 220 performances. Barba dissolved the company, concerned that the success of *Ferai* would distract the actors from training and developing their skills and understanding of theatre. Barba was concerned that the actors would only live for performance rather than live for theatre. He set out new contracts for the actors that emphasised the training aspects of the work and some of the performers did not rejoin the company. During the first ten years in Holstebro the emphasis of the Odin activities was on converting the farm buildings into performance and training spaces, training themselves and organising seminars and workshops from guest performers. Many of these practitioners, such as Jerzy Grotowski, Dario **Fo** and Jacques **Lecoq** had international reputations while others like I Made **Djimat** from Bali and Sanjukta **Panigrahi** from India were scarcely known outside their own countries. NTL was, and is, very much involved with documenting the work: editing and publishing material about theatre and the art of the actor in magazines, books and on video. The work that they have been involved in and organised has always been eclectic and drawn on the skills and expertise of practitioners from many parts of the world and from many genres of performance: clowning, mime, political theatre and dance-drama. As well as using the exercises that Barba had seen Grotowski's actors using in Opole, he sought advice and prompted his actors to read and research widely. Examples of approaches to acting from books by the great European theatre practitioners such as Stanislavsky, Meyerhold, **Craig** and **Copeau** were studied. The actors were also encouraged to work from pictures of **Kabuki** performers and **Beijing Opera** in their training, as well as listen to vocal music from around the world. All of this research was part of their dramaturgy and helped them to develop physical and vocal exercises that challenged their understanding of the potential of the voice and body, beyond its everyday use.

By the early 1970s the Odin had an established reputation in Europe for its innovative repertoire and developing style of performances, but Odin was also considered to be an important site of cultural debate across many areas of theatre. The practitioners, who came to the Odin Teatret to perform and give demonstrations of their craft, enabled the actors to directly experience the many forms of theatre practice that, previously, they had known only from pictures. As part of NTL the members of the company have continued to develop their own interests alongside the theatre work. For example, the actors Julia Varley, Torgeir Wethal and Iben Nagel Rasmussen have all developed their own projects in addition to the work they do as part of the Odin Teatret. Varley has been part of a women's performance collective called *The Magdalena Project* since 1986, and developed two additional branches of the work called *Transit* and *The Open Page* (a journal that actively encourages women theatre practitioners to write about their work). Wethal is a film-maker and has directed and edited a range of short films documenting the training and performances at Odin Teatret, and Rasmussen has set up her own theatre training school, Farfa.

## A 'SMALL TRADITION' AND TRAINING

As you can see from the account so far, training has always been central to the Odin practice. Training is considered to be a lifetime's pursuit whereby each member must identify, discover and surmount 'obstacles that hinder communication' (Barba, 1979: 35). What the company discovered was that this journey was different for each individual. There may be collective points of departure and a shared route, but each of us will find our own way. For the first 12 years, Barba observed and directed the actors' training each morning but, after this time, each actor trained alone. When Barba handed over the responsibility of training to each individual actor, the actors began to take on their own apprentices and became responsible for the training of new members, and so the company began to grow.

Training as an apprenticeship is usually concerned with learning skills and following an established tradition, but for the early Odin actors the apprenticeship was about finding their own way as they were making a tradition. The experienced actors in the company now have their 'small tradition', which they use as a basis for the initial training of their apprentices.

Barba describes Odin as an endogamous tribe, that is, an organism that grows from the inside. For example, Tage Larsen joined the company in 1972 and initially taught Julia Varley when he adopted her as his apprentice in 1976. They worked very hard training early each day before the Odin workday officially began. Barba was very clear that the Odin members were expected to work every day from seven in the morning, so if they wanted to train apprentices it must be in their own time. Tage worked with Julia for two years before Julia was fully adopted into the Odin tribe.

Latterly, Barba has discussed at length the development of the Odin's training in relation to learning the actor's craft in different cultures. When the company began they did not have a teacher or a prescribed approach or style to their craft. Initially, they needed to share what skills they had. In many cultural practices the performer chooses to train within a particular performance genre, for example ballet, **commedia dell'arte** or Kathakali, and he or she will often specialise in a particular role. The apprentice begins by learning to stand, sit, walk, use facial expression and their hands according to the particular discipline in which they have chosen to work. In life we learn these behaviours through a process known as **inculturation**, which is according to the necessary requirements or demands of our particular cultural context (people in colder climates, for example, occupy space and behave differently from people in hotter climates). The process of learning a particular mode of behaviour that is not everyday, for example ballet, is referred to as **acculturation**. The first phase of learning can often be very painful, physically and mentally. The body is forced into all manner of seemingly impossible positions that, at this stage, are also inexplicable. As Barba says, '[t]hey collide with the normal behaviour of the pupil's culture, biography, family circle, and experiences, deforming everything s/he has learned "naturally" through the painless process of inculturation' (Barba, 2000a: 264).

For the Odin actors the process of learning was further complicated by the fact that there was no model to aim towards: no perfected result to look up to. How would they know if they had achieved an appropriate level of competence to move onto the next stage of learning? For this reason the early years of their work are often referred to as a 'Closed Room' (see Christofferson, 1993), that is they trained behind closed doors. When a performer chooses to learn ballet s/he is joining a tradition, a collective identity. In contrast, Odin Teatret needed to create a collective identity and invent their 'small tradition'. A performer joining the company now, should they be invited, has many examples and a wealth of experiences to draw on from the older actors. Paradoxically, the Odin approach to actor training teaches that there is no single way to train, each of us must find our own way. What we can learn are the principles of learning and how we might best develop our learning.

In an article titled 'Tacit Knowledge' (2000a), Barba defines small traditions as those that are based on research at a 'trans-stylistic' level, a style that transcends any specific style or tradition. This idea of the 'trans-stylistic' connects with what Barba said earlier about the actor and the company both aiming to be a floating island by being transnational and transcultural, that is, not fixed or rooted in one cultural tradition. As we can begin to see, Odin's work corresponds to the definition of trans-stylistic, transnational and transcultural because, as Barba says:

> [t]hey do not try and pass on a style which corresponds to the tastes of the founders, or a new and original codification, but the roots of the craft, those principles of scenic behaviour which permit choices in the most diverse artistic directions.

(Barba, 2000a: 273)

## ODIN AND THE IDEA OF 'THIRD THEATRE'

Odin has developed a particular way of making and performing theatre derived from their wide range of experiences and research. Barba states that while the company has lots of advice that it can offer, Odin does not hold itself up as a model. However, Odin is a concrete example of how, through passion, commitment and discipline, a group of people can make theatre work. Through theatre they have built a small society of people with different social and political views but who all share a deep respect for their craft. Even in their early stages, Barba referred to the company as a 'little society', what he now refers to as their 'small tradition', or '**Third Theatre**'. By 'Third Theatre' he means that their theatre is neither what might be called avant-garde or experimental, nor traditional, that is, part of a cultural institution. While their training has always been concerned with experimentation it is not experimental, in the sense that it is not concerned with challenging the boundaries of what might be considered acting. Its aim is to research, consolidate and refine the actor's craft. Similarly, the approach to the performance work was established very early on in the life of the company. Subsequently, although spectators not familiar with the style might find the performance work challenging, the company would not consider the work to be experimental. The company sets itself very high standards for both their training and performance work, which are consistently rigorous and demand a discipline that is exacting. Barba states that the company's aims were to find a new theatrical language, new forms of contact with the spectator (Barba, 1979: 29) and to develop a theatre not rooted in one cultural tradition but a 'theatre that dances', that is, a theatre not wholly dependent on spoken text but employing dance and song. The developments in the theatre performance, like the developments in the training, work within a framework of existing knowledge. The aim is to develop that knowledge, not to create new knowledge.

## 'THIRD THEATRE' AS A GLOBAL NETWORK

'Third Theatre' is a term that Barba uses to describe those theatre companies around the world that choose to do things differently from the mainstream, the traditional and the institutional. He first began to use the term in 1976 at a conference in Belgrade. That conference also served as a meeting point for theatre groups that Barba had met on his travels. What emerged from this meeting was that there were shared traits among these and other groups around the world. These theatre companies exist outside of the mainstream, they are often formed by people who do not have a formal training so, although they are not amateurs, they are not considered professionals. These theatre groups would not define themselves as avant-garde or experimental, as their intention is not to 'make it new'. These companies are not fed on large subsidies and have to fight to find audiences for their performances. They are often based outside of large metropolitan areas. Their work is often devised, created by the group of performers, not scripted by a playwright outside of the company, and is not work that might be seen performed by other companies in later years. They make theatre for themselves, not for trends or fashions, and develop a style that is recognised as their identity. These companies exist everywhere, for the most part unnoticed by critics and academic scrutiny. Their work is fuelled by necessity and abhors indifference, and resists incorporation to the centre of what Barba refers to as 'planet theatre' (1991: 5). Early papers on the subject of 'Third Theatre' warned that it was not a category and that its only defining feature was 'recognition of discrimination that many theatre groups live under' (Barba, 1999b: 176). Barba recounts the beginnings of Odin Teatret to illustrate what he means by discrimination. The founding members of Odin were a group of young people without experience or training, who had been refused entry to the legitimate theatre school and, by necessity, had to start out alone. In addition, they could not find a permanent space to work until, after several years, an offer came from a small town without a theatre in a foreign country.

> We had to succeed in living this situation not as an impairment. We had to find a way of not yielding to the two handicaps that irredeemably prohibited us from doing a kind of theatre that, in those years, was recognised and accepted: the handicap of language, that prevented us from expressing ourselves theatrically through texts, and the handicap of our lack of theatrical education.
>
> (Barba, 1999b: 184)

What can emerge from those groups that survive and build a following, a small tradition, is a sense of independence that, later, Barba called a kind of resistance. By the 1990s Barba had re-evaluated what it was to be a 'Third Theatre' and considered the search for meaning to be a defining characteristic, rather than the experience of discrimination, as identified in papers and meetings in the 1970s and 1980s. 'Meaning', here, alludes to the search for a performance language that communicates to the spectator. The 'Third Theatre' may be defined precisely by its lack of a shared meaning: 'each [theatre company] defines its meaning and legacy by embodying them in a precise activity and through a distinct professional identity' (Barba, 1991: 7).

## THE TRAVELLING TIME

During the latter part of the 1970s the company took the opportunity to travel, meet with theatres working in a similar way to them, and observe and learn different performance practices, music and dance.

The second period of Odin's development began in 1974, when the company went to stay for five months in the rural village of Carpignano in Southern Italy. They went to the village to work on a new production that was to become *Come! And the Day will be Ours*. The landscape and remoteness of the community worked as a stimulus for them, but it also confronted them with questions as to their professional identity and purpose. They did not have a performance to perform for the local residents of the village, so when the inhabitants asked them who they were and they replied 'actors', they were not able to prove their identity. The dilemma of what they could offer the villagers of Carpignano led to the first barter, or performance exchange. From the experience in Carpignano, Odin have continued to develop many street performances, clowning, parades and many barters with the communities that they have visited. To this day, barters and street performance remain a central aspect of the company's work wherever they go (*Negotiating Cultures* (2002), edited by Ian Watson, has a very informative and interesting section on the barter work developed by Barba and Odin). *Anabasis* (first performed in 1977) is a good example of a street performance; the performance later provided characters and material that were developed further as a part of the indoor production *The Million*.

The outdoor performances and parades are highly organised works that look to theatricalise public space. They are structured as a series of scenarios that can be experienced and made sense of as individual sections but each section also connects to the other scenes and the whole performance; what might also be understood as a **montage** (see **scenic**

**montage**). Barba is still very much the director of the final performance although, as the actors have said, the outdoor performances often need a higher degree of organisation by the whole team. This is because there are so many more variables when working outside than with the indoor events, for example, their performances are constantly shifting from free **improvisation** with a **score** to a fixed rehearsed score.

The aim is to transform the public space and invite spectators to see their environment in a new and different way. The work uses many different levels from the street to balconies and the rooftops of buildings. Street performance will also seek out and use unfamiliar places that, maybe, the spectator does not usually look at. The characters Odin developed are larger than life, often walking on stilts; they are noisy, colourful and always entertaining. The performances are not stationary and the audience is all around, often not knowing where the front or the back of the performance might be. The spectator can be on the edge of the action one moment and in the midst of the action the next. Some of the action is performed up close to spectators and some at a distance but all the spectators must feel included all of the time; for the actors this has entailed them having to learn particular skills and techniques to engage the spectators. Characters that the actors have created for the outdoor performances have also travelled indoors, for example Anabasis, Geronimo and Mr Peanut are all characters who began 'life' in street performances but who have also appeared in indoor theatre performances. These characters have grown with the actors who created them and are still being adapted for performances in the Odin repertoire.

As a consequence of the experiences of performing in public spaces, the company re-evaluated where the audience should be seated for their indoor performances: the audience is now usually positioned on two sides of a space, sitting opposite each other. This seating arrangement makes particular demands on the actor. The actors, says Barba, must be like Egyptian friezes or cubist art, directing communication in more than one direction and ensuring that the actor is focused and 'alive', otherwise the spectator will become more interested in the opposing spectators who are 'really' reacting!

Barba says that the actor should be omnipotent, one who gives the illusion that they can be everywhere and anywhere, seemingly invisible to the audience but actually always present. This aim has influenced the scenic decisions and lighting – for example, only a part of the performer's body might be illuminated, like in a **Rembrandt** painting. The lighting design also allows the actor to move around in darkness as though invisible. Usually Odin does not work with a scenic designer, as the emphasis for the design is always that it should be efficient: functional, easy to transport, set up and dismantle. Their aim is always to have a show that the company can set up in eight hours.

## ISTA: THE INTERNATIONAL SCHOOL OF THEATRE ANTHROPOLOGY

Barters, the emerging idea of the 'Third Theatre', and the concept of the floating islands were ideas that were all brought together and formed the initial idea for theatre anthropology in 1979. Barba had observed, while they had been travelling and performing, that a major aspect of their work was concerned with how to transmit an experience from life to performance. This issue led to Barba's involvement with theatre anthropology and to the formation in 1980 of ISTA, the International School of Theatre Anthropology. ISTA is defined as, 'a multicultural network of performers and scholars giving life to an itinerant university whose main field of study is Theatre Anthropology' (Hastrup, 1996: 7). 'Theatre Anthropology: First Hypothesis' was a paper presented by Barba at a conference in Warsaw in 1980. In this first paper, Barba defines theatre anthropology as 'the study of human behaviour on a biological and socio-cultural level in a performance situation' (Barba, 1986a: 115). The definition has since been altered and refined in relation to the research undertaken under the auspices of ISTA (see Chamberlain, 2000). To date, the definition stands more simply as a comparison of working processes outside of the performance situation. The following chapter will explore in more detail what Barba considers to be the main concerns of theatre anthropology.

The first meeting of ISTA was in Bonn, Germany, in October 1980, and lasted four weeks. There have been 13 ISTA sessions to date, the last held in Germany in 2000. Each session focuses on a specific area of study. For example, the 1986 session, held in Holstebro, was titled 'The Female Role as Represented on the Stage in Various Cultures'. The 1995 session held in Umeå, Sweden, was titled 'Form and Information' (see Hastrup, 1996, for a complete list of the first ten years). The sessions have been reduced from the four weeks of the first session to approximately two weeks. The first section of the session is closed to the public and is for those invited artistic and scientific staff, and a selection of participants who applied and were selected to attend. The final three or four days are usually an open public symposium of discussions, work demonstrations and performances. The work conducted at ISTA will be looked at in more detail in Chapter 3 in relation to the Theatrum Mundi Ensemble's performance *Ego Faust*. For the first few sessions of ISTA the final performance was known as *Theatrum Mundi*. The performance has had many different guises and is refined and developed each time it is performed. Members of the Odin Teatret and many of the performers and musicians who have contributed their expertise as artistic staff at ISTA, all perform together in a piece directed by Eugenio Barba.

The work undertaken at ISTA has often led to controversy, most notably at the session held in 1986 titled 'The Female Role as Represented on the Stage in Various Cultures'. Here, many of the women attending the event as participants were very concerned that predominantly male performers were demonstrating the female roles. Critics such as Erica Munk (1986), Phillip Zarrilli (1988) and Marco De Marinis (1995) have questioned many aspects of theatre anthropology and the research status of ISTA, even going as far as accusing Barba of 'cultural imperialism' by way of imposing his ideology and training methodologies on other cultures. Barba refutes the accusations made against him, saying that he has sought to depersonalise his observations of the performance work and training, both at Odin and in theatre work he has encountered on his travels. This reflective position, he says, has guided him towards developing the concept of theatre anthropology through the research undertaken at ISTA. The techniques encountered in other cultural practices have, for example, led Barba to re-evaluate his thinking and understanding of scenic behaviour. Scenic behaviour is a term adopted by Barba and Odin to describe the work and techniques of the performer's extra-daily behaviour, an acculturated behaviour that constitutes their 'small tradition' and performance practice. The idea that theatre is an expression of cultural identity has been a problem for Barba, as he does not wholly agree with the idea that performance is culturally bound. He believes this idea is too generalised and assumes a cultural homogeneity, that is, it suggests that members of a culture, and their cultural practices, are all the same and this is not what he has observed in his research. However, what Barba has observed are common underlying principles, at what he calls a **pre-expressive** level, that are evident in performance practices from many different cultures, for example the use of energy. For Barba, performance and actors should be transcultural and transnational, so not rooted in a particular culture. Theatre anthropology tries to find neutral territory to discuss performance processes. Too often, he says, we look to comment on form and content when we should focus on form and information. The evolution of the term pre-expressive came from the form of the work that the 'artists' at ISTA produced and what Barba noticed in the performers' scenic behaviour, exercises and demonstrations. Barba also noticed that a student attending the ISTA as a participant often appeared to find the learning environment very difficult, especially when trying to learn another cultural practice, for example **Noh** Theatre, and this was because s/he was looking at the content and not the form. In an attempt to solve the problem of how we learn, Barba identified three principles that appeared to underpin what he called extra-daily behaviour and they are: alteration of balance, the law of opposition as refined in art, and incoherent coherence or **equivalence**. These three principles, Barba argues, are common to all forms of scenic behaviour and we will explore what these might mean to us in practice in Chapters 2 and 4. Barba uses the metaphor of the police investigator at the scene of a crime to illustrate the use of theatre anthropology. He says that although the investigator will not know who the criminal might be, they will know how to investigate; so, theatre anthropology allows a **concrete** process of investigation for the performer.

Barba and Odin have travelled extensively and worked with a wide range of performers from many different performance practices. All this experience has led to the development of Third Theatre, ISTA and, more recently, Eurasian Theatre. At the gatherings of these different groups the intention is not to compare results but the processes of working.

## EURASIAN THEATRE

As an offshoot of ISTA, Eurasian Theatre is a summer school founded in collaboration with the University of Bologna, Italy, in 1990. The school meets annually in Italy and holds practical/theoretical sessions for participants to explore and discuss specific aspects of theatrical practice. Similar concerns are explored in the Eurasian Theatre sessions to those identified through the ISTA research: what lies beneath the surface of a performance practice? what constitutes the 'tradition of traditions'? (Barba, 1999a: 251). Barba defines Eurasian Theatre as exploring 'the movement between East and West' (1995: 42). He had noticed that although the Odin Teatret had developed their theatre identity from an autodidactic basis, from a basis of being self-taught, their work had not fallen into many of the conventional theatrical expectations that other European theatres have had. For example, European theatre has separated out dance from drama, whereas many non-European theatres do not recognise this as a divide, and Barba was interested in why this should be the case. The function of Eurasian Theatre is to create a space where, from what Kirsten Hastrup calls a 'zero point of perception' (Hastrup, 1996: 95), we can explore our professional theatre identity in the context of the complex root system that is theatre. Again, like ISTA, the study has not been developed to reinforce a value system that one practice is better than another but to encourage a better understanding of different practices, so that we can appreciate the diversity of theatre practices from around the world. The name Eurasian Theatre references those theatre traditions from Europe and Asia that have had a significant impact on our theatre today, for example **Artaud** was influenced by what he saw of Balinese theatre, **Brecht** was influenced by Japanese theatre and Stanislavsky was influenced by Chinese theatre. There are particular genres of performance from Asia that have, through history, shaped theatre in Europe. Eurasian Theatre creates a space where these genres can be studied, not only historically or as traditions but, as already said, for what lies beneath the surface of the tradition.

## FESTUGE

The necessity to remain foreign, to be a floating island that does not put down roots in a particular culture, may suggest that Barba is not interested in culture. Although he advocates a theatre that transcends cultural specificity and encourages the development of an identity that is formed from living in the theatre rather than a society, he also celebrates cultural diversity. The move to Holstebro foregrounded the problems of making theatre as foreigners and, fundamentally, how, as performers, they engage the attention of the spectator. Meaning and literal understanding have never been the basis of the relationship between spectator and performer in the Odin Teatret.

Throughout the 36 years that Odin have been resident in Holstebro they have always considered the local community to be of the utmost importance. They have been sensitive to the fact that the theatre has attracted many overseas visitors who have, at times, overwhelmed the community. Despite the Odin's international reputation and gruelling schedule of overseas tours, the group, when at home, takes perform-ances and workshops out to local schools and groups, and in more recent years they have become involved with the annual Festuge.

The Festuge was first held in Holstebro in 1989. It is a festival organ-ised by Odin involving many community organisations, participating and collaborating together with members of Odin Teatret and international performers, friends of Odin, invited to come and contribute perform-ances for, and with, the residents of Holstebro. Barba describes it as 'an orgy of barters' (1999b: 97). A centrepiece of the third Festuge held in September 1993 was a production of the Sanskrit play *Shakuntala*. This intercultural production was directed by Barba and involved the Odin actors, Sanjukta Panigrahi and her musicians from India, members of the Holstebro Music School, Danish Opera singers, guest appearances from the Peruvian theatre company Yuyachkani, and the Italian company Teatro Tascabile. Each evening of the Festuge an episode of the story would be performed in the town's library. During the day there would be numerous events, performances, parades and exhibitions taking place all over the town.

## WHAT IS IT TO BE AN ACTOR?

Already, the map of Eugenio Barba and Odin Teatret's career is complex. The map embraces many parts of the world, many people and many events. The journey so far has merely marked the route and needs now to consider how the work functions.

During the **Odin Week** in March 2001, Barba identified four ques-tions that a performer needs to ask, stressing that there are no formulaic answers. He ruled that it was for each individual to make his or her own response. The questions are:

How do I become an effective actor?

Why make theatre and not something else?

Where are you going to do the theatre?

For whom are you doing the theatre – who are your spectators?

(Odin Week, 2001)

Historically, the actor has worked to develop characters from stock characters: archetypes that are not psychologically motivated. Western theatre, at the beginning of the twentieth century, began to disrupt and subvert the archetypal notion of character. Theatre, along with many other traditional forms of art at this time, was challenged in the **modernist** cry of 'make it new'. In the theatre this was urged on by what Barba argues was a reaction to the mediocrity of theatre at the time. The new exponents of European theatre believed in a theatre that could transcend what they saw as the banality of society. Significantly, it was at this point that theatre shifted from being considered merely as a form of entertainment to being an art form. Theatre was changing and demanded a new style of actor. The new breed of actor was required to start with the self at a point of zero in order to transform her or himself into an imitation of the playwright's character.

Barba has not been seeking to reverse this trend but he does approach the actor's craft with a different set of principles. The precision of exercises, performances and terminology has always been vitally important. Part of Barba's and the Odin actors' research has been focused on finding terms that will communicate their experiences and observations, both to other practitioners and outside observers, thus facilitating discussion and debate about the craft of the actor. The following part of this chapter will introduce particular terms used by Barba in relation to the Odin approach to training and dramaturgy.

## TRAINING SEASONS AND SCORES

At the Odin Teatret, as with the Russian theatre practitioner Meyerhold's theatre and Grotowski's laboratory, there has always been a clear distinction between the function of exercises in training and in the work of the rehearsal. The function of exercises, and what we understand improvisation to mean, are areas that will be explored in Chapters 3 and 4. The point to be noted here is that Odin made a virtue out of not knowing how to train or rehearse and, as a consequence, they have learnt to reflect, research and evaluate every step that they have taken. They have developed an informed understanding of their craft; nothing that the actor does is taken for granted, everything is observed and reflected upon. Barba has been adamant that the craft of the actor should not be veiled in mystique but should be worked at and discussed, always in concrete terms.

Barba acknowledges the major influence both Meyerhold and Stanislavsky have had, not only on his work as a director but also on the development of the actor's craft. Notably, both practitioners identified that the smallest perceptible phrase visible to the spectator is always a reaction and must be consciously performed. A performance should always engage the whole body of the performer, as even the smallest action has the potential to change the perception of the spectator.

The early training undertaken at Odin is illustrated in the two films directed by Torgeir Wethal, *Physical Training at Odin Teatret* and *Vocal Training at Odin Teatret*, both made in 1972. Commenting on the films, Barba notes that training by repetition can be in danger of creating mannerisms in the actor. Having observed the actors repeating exercises daily, Barba saw that what was needed was to teach them not to act but to reflect and think. He emphasises the work on 'real' actions based in fiction. It is the quality of the action that makes it 'real'; Barba uses a boxing exercise to demonstrate what he means. By boxing with an actor using only illustrative movements, or pantomime, the quality of the movements and the energy is empty. The other actor has nothing to react and respond to. In order for the action to be 'real' there must be, what Barba calls, **sats**, which is an impulse to move. An action that is real forces the actor to react with their whole body. The action does not begin when the punch lands on the opponent but the action begins in the readiness and alertness of the opponent. If the action is not precise and clearly indicated, the other actor cannot respond or react, and then the performance cannot be real. In pairs, try the boxing exercise that Barba discusses above. First, pretend with your partner that you are in a boxing match and play it in a pantomime style. You have no intention of hitting each other but give the illusion that you are fighting. Reflect on where your energy has been focused and whether you had both been totally engaged with the exercise. Where were you looking? Were you well balanced on the ground? Who was leading the boxing?

Now try to use real actions; you will need to be very alert and take care, otherwise you will actually be hit! Note how this time you need to be well balanced, you need to be looking at your partner all the time, you need to be thinking ahead. You need to use sats to prepare to respond to your partner. Now reflect on what you need to do to keep the quality of energy, spontaneity and alertness in the performance of this action. As performers, we are often required to choreograph our moves and fix them precisely. This technique can dull an actor's senses and consequently lead to a dull performance.

Technique can be a problem for the actor when it is treated like armour, or something we hide behind. The actor's story is expressed through the actions that he or she makes, so if they are hiding behind an armoury of technique their story and actions will be dulled. They must melt the armour to penetrate beyond it and make real actions and find real responses to impulses, like with the boxing exercise. The same alert relationship that occurs between two actors should also be present between an actor and a spectator. Barba describes this sense of alertness demanded of actors as, 'being decided'.

Although we began this section indicating that there is a distinct difference between training and rehearsal, the actor participates in both activities. A central dilemma that Barba has identified through the years of his work, but has not been able to fully resolve, is that some actors are not good performers but are very good in training, and some actors are very bad in training but good performers. He has concluded that, although there appears to be no connection between the quality of performance and the quality of training, the emphasis for all actors must be on training his or her potential **scenic presence**. Training scenic presence requires working on exercises that engage the whole body and that will serve both the body in exercise and the body in performance. For Odin actors, a key question in their training is how to give the impression of life in their work – as demonstrated in the boxing exercise – and how they can continue to develop their scenic presence.

Odin actors look to make action extra-daily, that is, separate their everyday behaviour from their performance behaviour. The behaviour they each develop is formalised and codified, which means that each action they make is precise. Precision is determined and recorded as a score by the actor and will include the size of the action, the position of the body, the breathing, the focus of the eyes. In many ways, the actor's score is similar to a choreographic score or a musical composition but, unlike most choreographies, the movements are not abstract and the score is not just a physical score; most importantly it is also a mental score. Score is a term frequently used by Barba and the Odin actors to describe a sequence of actions. Montage is another term that they use to describe the way in which scores might be developed and put together. There are various terms that are used frequently by Barba when he is talking about actor training. Take the opportunity to check in the glossary terms such as scenic presence, pre-expressive, extra-daily, sats, score and montage if they are unfamiliar.

As noted previously, Grotowski's work initially informed the training at Odin but after a couple of years the exercises no longer functioned as a challenge to the actors and had to be transformed by the actors into part of their personal training. As Barba said earlier, exercises are like bricks and can be put together to build different things. Meyerhold's advice and approach to actor training was also influential, not only on the Odin approach to training but also on the way that they prepared for performance. Meyerhold states that the spoken score should be prepared and worked on separately from the physical score. This has the effect of creating two different logics or narratives that will both correspond to a central theme but not necessarily explicitly to each other, except on the level of the actor's internal score. The following exercise may serve as an example of how an internal score works. In a group of three, choose a fairy tale that you know. Your task is to physically construct an account of the fairy tale using only your hands to tell the story. As a group, agree on the key actions that you each will use to tell the story. Next, construct your version of the story using these actions. Ensure you engage your whole body physically in the task, although it is only your hands that are telling the story. Even if the actions are very small they should be precise and engage the whole body. Once this task has been achieved separate out the group, and make three new groups. Repeat your actions in your new group. This time each individual is performing their actions dissociated from the rest of the story but each individual has an internal score, which means that each person knows what they are doing and why they are doing it.

Meyerhold's approach to constructing a performance score is key to understanding how the Odin actors create and perform characters. The characters are not psychologically motivated, in the Stanislavskian sense, but are governed by the physical, vocal and internal scores created by the actors. Chapter 4 will introduce you to further ways that a performance score might be generated.

The seminars and work demonstrations that the actors have developed for other student actors reflect their own personal experiences and are often autobiographical and anecdotal in presentational style. They do not teach techniques in a didactic manner but invite participants to reflect on their own experiences and evaluate what they have learnt and how they have chosen to train and perform. 'Why act?' has always been the starting point for Barba.

Roberta Carreri, an actor with Odin since 1974, has created a work demonstration called *Traces in the Snow* that documents how her training has developed (see also Carreri, 2000). She is now in what she calls her 'third season' of training. For her this meant that she could begin to develop her own physical scores: make her own solo performances. A solo performance offered Roberta Carreri a new set of challenges in both her training and performance work. Incorporating performance practices from Japan, China, Bali and India determined the agenda for her 'third season' of training. The 'first season' of training involved being taught by older colleagues in the group. For Carreri, her first season lasted for three years. Kai Bredholt, who is at present the newest member of the company, has been in his 'first season' of training for 11 years but now is moving into his 'second season'. His 'second season' entails working with other performers and practitioners outside of the company in order to develop his own style of performance. It is important to stress that, although the Odin actors all work very closely together, they each have a very different style of performance, and this is very evident in their work demonstration *Whispering Winds*.

When the actor takes responsibility for her/his own training s/he moves into the 'second season'. S/he needs to identify particular principles that will be central to her/his work. Inspiration for the work may be found in the work of other practitioners, in books, in paintings, or in photographs, as we have already noted. All the time the composition of the body needs to be fully understood so that it may be constantly challenged. Roberta Carreri notes that it is important to have constructed a fixed frame of rules that will govern practical exercises and training each day that you work. Often, we experience an overwhelming sense of fatigue when exercising. An exercise can quickly become dull, not because the body is tired but because the brain is not

being engaged. We need to constantly seek out new stimuli and challenges within exercises, both for the mind and the body. Chemicals
released in the body, such as endorphins, enable us to overcome the
obstacle of tiredness that the body sets up. We each need to explore
the well of energy that is our body so that we can engage the endorphins and overcome fatigue and, consequently, achieve a greater depth
in our training work. In the work demonstration, *Traces in the Snow*,
Carreri shows how an exercise can be changed through intensity, size
and direction. Focusing on specific parts of the body, for example, the
eyes, hands, or feet can give us an awareness of how different body
parts can be articulated separately. Carreri has worked in this way to
identify how the spectator's attention may be directed in specific ways:
the feet may be doing one thing and telling one story while the eyes
may be doing something contrasting and different, that is, telling a
different story. You might try this as an exercise using two different
fairy tales. In a similar way that you told the story of a fairy tale using
only your hands, in the exercise above (see page 28), choose a second
fairy tale and build a way of telling the story using only your eyes. When
you have done this, try performing both stories at the same time. It is
imperative that the beginning of an exercise is marked, that it has a
developed form and a precise end.

For Carreri, training has frequently involved improvising with exercises that she has created or adapted from other exercises that she has
seen. These improvisations, although initiated in training, can also be
useful when preparing for a new performance. Through improvisation,
images can be spontaneously generated that can later be developed into
a montage or form the basis of a score. Rather than sitting and talking
about an improvisation, this approach entails working and playing spontaneously. The actor's imaginative internal stories, or internal score,
that enable the actor to recall his or her external actions with precision, are one way of fixing the images evolved from improvisation. Even
if the director changes the external context of a montage, the actor is
able to keep the actions precise, as his or her internal story will remain
the same. For example, the actor may present a sequence of action and
the director might ask the actor to perform the sequence as though they
are in the midst of a wild storm. The action would need to be modified but the internal story, that is invisible to the director and spectator,
remains the same. Once you have a fixed score of actions you can colour
the actions in many and varied ways. If you return again to the sequence

of actions that made up your score for the fairy tale you can see how this sequence is precise and fixed. You can now colour the score in any way you choose. For example, try performing your score with different colours, or qualities: as though in a wild storm, as though you are trying not to be caught moving, or as though trying to communicate with someone a long way away. Each time it is only the outer actions that are modified but your internal story should remain the same.

When discussing the building process of a performance Barba is careful to always begin with the spectator. He says that although there can be no general message contained within a performance, as each spectator hears something different, there are key ideas and realities that are **embodied** by a culture in a particular time and space, and these ideas and realities might constitute a shared understanding on a general level.

## DRAMATURGY

The term dramaturgy is applied in different ways in different theatrical contexts. Barba refers to the dramaturgy of the actor, the dramaturgy of the director and the dramaturgy of the spectator. The term is defined as deriving from the Greek, *drama-ergon*, and 'refers to the inner or invisible energy of an action. An action is a work, an activity. The dramaturgy of a performance is the way an action is told or shown and becomes functional as dramatic energy' (Christofferson, 1993: 125). For the actor, the dramaturgy may be the necessary research that has informed and prepared an action or sequence that gives it an 'inner or invisible energy'. Dramaturgy is a term that is common to the theatres in many parts of Europe and America but is not so well known in Britain. Brecht, for example, worked with a team of dramaturgs at the Berliner Ensemble. These people were not performers but were researchers and produced materials that aided the actors and director in their work during the rehearsal process. Often, the term references the literary text alone but, in the case of Odin Teatret, dramaturgy operates as an 'organic or dynamic dramaturgy' (Barba, 2000b: 60). This 'organic or dynamic dramaturgy' is not directed at the spectator's ability to understand a performance in terms of its meaning but the range of experiences it might offer using all the theatrical elements, from the vocal and physical score, the costumes, the music, through to the props. The spectator's dramaturgy is constructed through the experience of the performance, the connections that each individual makes in relation to the many threads that are woven together by the performers to create a sense of coherence. A performance should not intend to make a meaning explicit but should intend to create spaces where the spectator may question the potential and available meanings in the performance. Barba sees the performance as 'the beginning of a longer experience' (Barba, 1990: 98) for the spectator. As spectators, we may not have been able to follow all the possible readings available in a performance in the moment of its performance, but we may reflect on it for months, even years, after the performance. In his article 'Four Spectators' (1990) Barba considers his role as director to be that of the first spectator. Barba identifies different modes of response and interpretation that the spectator may experience. Barba calls these 'four "basic" spectators':

the child who perceives the actions literally;

the spectator who thinks s/he doesn't understand but who, in spite of her/himself dances, that is enjoys the performance;

the director's alter-ego;

the fourth spectator who sees through the performance as if it did not belong to the world of the ephemeral and of fiction.

(Barba, 1990: 99)

The director's task is to recognise the needs of each spectator and weave a performance that will embrace each of their positions.

In Barba's theatre all the participants fulfil the role of dramaturg. From the beginning, performances at the Odin Teatret have been developed through the use of improvisation, even in the very early performances when they were working from a literary text. The mainstay of the group's work has been developed from ideas, themes and stories initially provided by Barba. The actors' dramaturgy is the score and **subscore** built through their response to the director's initial material using improvisation. The process of generating material for a performance has been developed to allow the actor to individually create their physical score separately from their vocal score. The materials used to build the physical score may be very different from material that builds the vocal score and this can lead to the actor's score appearing disjointed or disjunctive. Even in performance, the individual scores may still appear to be ambiguous or incoherent to the spectator, as energy appears to shoot off in different directions. The actors work on their improvisations alone, as Barba believes that their focus should be on their particular response to the material that has been presented and not on how they might work with the other actor(s) in the space. Barba comments that when improvising with a partner you have to work in real time and the work can often be merely illustrative. When working alone, time and reactions often appear to work differently; the actor can go much further alone as he or she inhabits what Barba calls the realm of 'dreaming awake' (Odin Week, 2001).

At a later stage, when each actor has constructed her/his score, s/he will then begin the process of weaving their scores together under the direction of Barba. The score must be embodied – another term often used by Barba – so that it can be repeated without having to think what comes next. Every detail of the score must be embodied, not just as a series of moves but also in terms of where the action comes from, how it is expressed, how the energy is being controlled and directed, where the breath comes, the size, tempo and rhythm of the action. Barba begins to work with the actor's score, modifying it in terms of space and articulation. For example, he might change the order in which the actions are expressed or the spatial dimension. He will also ensure that all unnecessary movements or gestures have been eliminated from the composition and that the actor's daily mannerisms have been removed. The score must be made up of actions not movements. Barba explains:

a 'physical action' is the 'smallest perceptible action' and is recognizable by the fact that even if you make a microscopic movement (the tiniest displacement of the hand, for example), the entire tonicity of the body changes. A real action produces change in the perception of the spectator.

(Barba, 1997: 128)

For Barba, the most essential aspect of the actor's craft is the way in which they are able to continually attract the attention of the spectator.

The dramaturgy of the director constructs sequences of actions woven from the performance scores prepared by the actors. For Barba, as the director, an important question to ask is how the performance might problematise the experience for the spectator. One way in which this might be done is by disrupting the viewing position for the spectator, and this is evidenced in the productions *Mythos* (1998) and *Kaosmos* (1993) where many things are happening simultaneously, forcing the spectator to create their own montage by choosing what they will give their attention to (see Figure 1.2). Simultaneity is a particular device used by Odin and many other contemporary theatre companies. Simultaneity occurs when the actor can represent several things at the same time; different actors occupying different fictional spaces within the same performance space can present many aspects of a story at the same time. Another way in which the normal viewing position can be disrupted in performance is illustrated in a solo perform-ance by Roberta Carreri titled *Judith* (1987). Here, different areas of the stage represent different parts of Judith's mind and the balance of the objects in the space are intentionally asymmetrical, so that we as spectators are disorientated and are invited to question, or alter, our perception of what is in the space. The dramaturgical process in *Judith* is described as dynamic and not narrative (this is illustrated in the work demonstration *Whispering Winds*).

As a director who has to prepare actors, Barba states that he must be interested in process. As a director he is dependent on what the actor proposes from the given materials, he is not like the American director Robert **Wilson**, who is renowned for his clear formalised vision of the performance before rehearsals have begun. Barba builds a pathway through the performance materials offered by the actors. He then sculpts the actors' work for the spectator.

It is important to note that there are essential differences between the dramaturgy of the actors and the dramaturgy of the director that continue through the rehearsal process to the final performance. Barba's role is to protect the performance text but not the means by which it was constructed by the actors. The dramaturgy that he constructs should be viewed as a succession of events that can be built separately and then placed within a structure that flows for the spectator. The performance text, although made up of many different parts, each contributed by one of the performers, must always have a clear context and Barba provides that. The relationship between the actors' different texts or scores might be considered as contiguous, that is the actors have a closeness in space and/or time to the theme, and sometimes actual contact with each other, but at the same time remain separate, thus creating layers and textures in the performance. The actors do not illustrate the theme or the characters but respond to them with their own associations.

**Figure 1.2** Roberta Carreri, Julia Varley, Tage Larsen and Iben Nagel Rasmussen in *Mythos*, 1993. Photograph by Jan Rüsz

Barba will often begin work on a new performance by meeting with the actors and giving them a theme that will act as a framework for them to improvise within. The theme needs to be concrete for them, something they can explore rather than illustrate. Barba gives an example of improvising with an idea, suggesting the theme for an improvisation as 'The man who knows there are no walls behind him'. Barba warns that we should not begin with the idea that there are walls behind. First, what needs to be explored is the idea of what is behind the walls, but not like in pantomime with a mimed illustration of the walls, but as real actions and reactions. Improvisation has always been a mainstay of the Odin toolbox. Improvisation is used to generate material in the preparation of all their new work. Barba collects materials that he considers to have a relationship to the ideas and themes he wants the production to explore, and some of these he will share with the actors. Barba would not give an improvisation specifically themed to the production, but one that has a lateral or enigmatic relationship to the theme, an emblematic image. His role as director is to seek out inner information that will give the actors a precise impulse to express the outer action. He needs to find improvisations that will lead him indirectly towards the theme. If 'uprooting' is the theme then he may request that the actors prepare an improvisation around the stimulus of following a map.

The actors prepare work for maybe a year on both their invisible, personal subscore and the visible score. Barba comes in to see the work, the visible score, and maybe he likes the work, maybe he does not. The actor continues to work until Barba sees something that he is interested in and then they will both work on developing the score. The final phase brings the whole company to work together in the performance space.

The performers' invisible subscores operate through the music, the costume, but mostly through 'a set of mental and kinaesthetic constructs, that form the preconditions which stimulate plausible responses made by the performer to fictitious situations' (Pavis, 1996b: no page numbers). This might be understood to be the images and associations stimulated for the actor by the source materials, that the actor has then structured together into their own personal narrative or score. The actors' actions, both physical and vocal, are intrinsically tied to their personal narrative and prevent the actions from being empty and mechanical.

## TO RECAP

So, we can see that for the Odin actors the process of constructing a performance entails creating a score drawn from many different stimuli, and that in order for the actor to fix the score, so that he or she can repeat it precisely each time with life and energy, the actor needs to have a means whereby all the associations, images, sounds, etc. can be re-gathered and remembered; this is the subscore. The subscore may have little, if any, literal relationship with the performance witnessed by the spectator. The other actors and Eugenio Barba do not need to know what constitutes the subscore or what it means; it is personal to the actor. The subscore does not need to have a rational logic but might have logic similar to dreams, coherent to the actor, although seemingly incoherent to anyone else. As we have noted earlier, the process of fixing the performer's score is similar to the process undertaken by a dancer learning a piece of dance choreography, but it entails not just a **dilation** of outer physical energy but also an internal mental dilation, referred to as embodying the score. The notion of embodying the score is a term frequently used by Barba and the Odin actors and refers to the level of knowing, again not solely on a mental level of knowing, but a level attained where both mind and body 'know'. Embodied is defined as being able to give expression to, or give tangible or visible form to, something abstract, and this is precisely what the actor is doing to their subscore. The score is embodied with the help of fixing the subscore; the actor's thoughts, actions and reactions can be refined in their expression of scenic presence. The performer, says Barba, needs to escape merely representing him or herself: 'a man is condemned to resemble a man, the body imitating itself' (Barba, 1995: 30), and this is not sufficient to be considered art. Scenic presence is the actor's craft of refining mundane, everyday behaviour into something that transcends mere imitation into theatrical art.

The approach to role at Odin might be better understood in terms of what it is not. It is in contrast to that which was sought by Stanislavsky's methodology: an interpretation of the motivations and psychology of a character. For the Odin actors, their response to a text is founded on their own associations; often the performances use objects and music that they have been given as gifts on their travels, so there is a sense that their theatre reflects an aspect of themselves as well.

The director, says Barba, can manipulate an emotionally effective impulse for the spectator, not in terms of a specific reading, but by enhancing or establishing a tone or emotional colour. The individual actor's score, as has been established, is a series of dynamic changes that, on its own, is not telling anything, not communicating anything for the audience yet and so can be treated as an exercise, although it has an internal narrative inscribed by the actor. The rehearsal process provides numerous difficulties for the Odin actor as, having fixed her or his score and subscore, Barba's role as director is to weave all the different scores together and create his own score. Barba's score constitutes the final performance. The actors will need to continually amend and adjust their scores as the final performance takes shape, this may entail reducing a sequence to the action of the eyes alone, or extending the score into a different spatial plane, reversing or reordering parts of the score; whatever the external changes might be, the actor needs to make corresponding adjustments to their internal score or subscore. The process of elaboration of the actor's initial score demands very detailed and precise work in order that the final score refines and synchronises the vocal and physical score in a negotiation between the actor and Barba.

Barba uses the metaphor of a perfume to illustrate the function of the performer's score. A perfume is made up from over 80 ingredients, some alone smell bad, some do not smell at all but together they create a perfume. The fixer used in perfume-making to enhance and fix the fragrance is like the score that can help all the other ingredients to mature over years.

## THE PRESENT

Barba has reflected that the Odin Teatret was built out of the ruins of Europe, that their innovative approach to training and performing developed, in part, because of the social and cultural disruption in Europe following the Second World War.

Barba describes himself and his actors as autodidactic, that is self-taught, and they have given, and continue to give, a life-long commitment to research into the art and craft of performing. On the frontispiece to *Beyond the Floating Islands* Barba quotes Niels Bohr: '[w]hatever I say should not be taken as an assertion but as a question' (Barba, 1986a). This quotation is a useful key to accessing Barba's writing and his approach to theatre practice and research. Barba is vitally important to continuing developments in performance practices because he offers the performer advice on how to transform him/herself beyond the merely representational.

At the beginning of the chapter we spoke of Barba's metaphor of 'two wounds'; Odin has always been aware of its status as a migrant company and the rejection that it might encounter. They needed to find, in this potential exclusion, a value and dignity through knowledge and technique. Barba has said that the excluded often accept their position, and he has shown that it needs courage to keep fighting, but it is essential to 'resist the grey routine as it kills' (Odin Week, 2001).

The Odin Teatret as it is now has been together over 40 years. When they started, the actors knew what it was to be hungry, as they had literally experienced rationing and the ruin of Europe and, metaphorically, the ruin of theatre. The young now, argues Barba, do not know hunger, they do not work, they do not prepare. They are like vampires who feed off their elders for short-term gain and would drain the life-blood from the Odin actors were it not for the fact that they no longer recruit and train apprentices. He has also said that he does not want to expand the company because the construction of the performances is a complicated process and when the 'tribe' increases its number from six to ten even, there are implications for Barba's work in the space, and the space the actors have to work in.

Theatrical tours of their work have, from an early period, included workshops and seminars; the Odin year is structured around periods of touring, periods of research, training, rehearsing and organising other events including seminars, Work Weeks, etc. They have always operated as a collective, whereby each member of the company earns the same wage and all contribute to the maintenance and cleanliness of the work-spaces; however, Barba is the leader and observers of the company may identify strong differences among the members of the company. As much as their work thrives as an example of ensemble practice, each individual asserts a strong individualism that is apparent in their work beyond the company, in their approach to training and their contribution to the performance style. The approach of this ensemble is not to make everyone the same but to celebrate each member's individualism. Being autodidactic, Odin members have each developed their own individual approach to training. They consider themselves, by necessity, foreigners and, as a consequence, and most importantly, have become, as Barba says, 'loyal to our diversity' (1988c: 128).

Odin will disappear in its material form when Barba and the actors leave but the work is already interwoven into the fabric of western theatrical genealogy. It is not that this 'small tradition' will be lost, but Odin Teatret is particular to Barba and cannot be replicated. It can be invented anew by directors and actors who may have been touched by the ideas and practices encountered at ISTA, in Holstebro, at an Odin performance, and intend to make their own way and create their own 'small tradition', contiguous, maybe, to the Odin Teatret.

The ideas and practices that have been explored may, on the surface, appear to be formulaic but Barba's approach comes with over 40 years' experience and Barba would want it stressed that we consider the ideas and approaches in this book as their way, and not a blueprint that if learnt and followed will reproduce the same results. The company are clear that they have no encompassing theory of the theatre, or the craft of the actor, just experiences and advice to share.

## A FINAL THOUGHT

It can sometimes make sense to confront a theory with a biography. My journey through cultures has heightened my sensorial awareness and honed my alert- ness, both of which have guided my professional work. Theatre allows me to belong to no place, to be anchored not to one perspective only, to remain in transition.

(Barba, 1995: 8)

# 2

# JOURNEYS
# BY CANOE

As we have seen in Chapter 1, Barba's aim is to make the craft of the actor as accessible as possible. That the craft of acting is visible and concrete and not veiled in mystique, is of the utmost importance to him. He achieves this aim both through practice, in workshops and demonstrations, and also through his writing. Although, as he says at the beginning of his book *The Paper Canoe*, 'the memory of experience lived as theatre, once translated into sentences that last, risks becoming petrified into pages that cannot be penetrated' (Barba, 1995: 12). Many of his papers and articles have been collected in volumes such as *The Floating Islands* (1979), *Beyond the Floating Islands* (1986a), *Land of Ashes and Diamonds* (1999a) and *Theatre: Solitude, Craft, Revolt* (1999b). In this chapter we will be looking principally at *The Paper Canoe: A Guide to Theatre Anthropology*, written in 1995, and also at *A Dictionary to Theatre Anthropology: The Secret Art of the Performer*, co-written with Nicola Savarese in 1991. Both of these texts document theatre anthropology as an area of research that has been developed over the ten or 15 years of meetings of the International School of Theatre Anthropology. The area of theatre anthropology is Barba's self-acknowledged obsession with trying to reveal what it is to act, which is to make the invisible visible. The research work that has been undertaken as theatre anthropology is important to both students and practitioners of theatre as it gives us a concrete basis from which we can observe and analyse what constitutes the craft of the actor. The two books work hand in hand to reveal 'the secret art of the performer' using annotated photographs and drawings, theatre history, observations from the ISTA sessions and accounts from the practitioners who have presented and demonstrated as part of ISTA sessions. The two books also record Barba's own observations, experiences and anecdotes from throughout his career. The books make reference to the 'Secret Art', 'the invisible made visible' and the 'anatomy of the actor' (an alternative title for Barba and Savarese's book). These terms all point us towards an exploration of what is beneath the surface of the actor's character and role. The principal concerns of theatre anthropology are not the performance aspects of theatre, the content and other visible forms, but the invisible forms where 'mental energy (invisible) becomes somatic energy (visible)' (Barba, 1988b: 12). Although many of the photographs in the dictionary show the performer in a performance mode, in costume and make-up, we are asked to look beyond the visible to what is beneath the surface. The form of the dictionary is useful as it gives concrete definitions to the terms developed through theatre anthropology, but, as with any dictionary, the definition or meaning of one term merely refers the reader to another term that is similar but may also need to be defined. In the case of this dictionary it is not words that are being defined but practices. Many of the definitions are illustrated by performance practices from many different cultures. Whereas *The Paper Canoe* (1995) is illustrated with written examples, the *Dictionary of Theatre Anthropology* (Barba and Savarese, 1991) is crammed with page after page of visual examples that serve to both whet our appetite to find out more about the theatre practices that they illustrate and aid in our understanding of what the field of theatre anthropology is concerned with. It is useful when reading *The Paper Canoe* to reference across the terms that Barba introduces and check what the *Dictionary of Theatre Anthropology* entry says and shows.

*The Paper Canoe* conjures up an image of a voyage, a journey in a vessel that is fragile. The journey the reader is taken on is both through time and space, as Barba draws on theatre practitioners and practices from the past and from across the world. The ideas, reflections and thoughts are presented using different forms of writing; for example, chapters four and six are made up of a series of notes and chapter eight includes a letter, and has a detailed account of workshop activities. Throughout the book Barba tells us stories, recounts experiences, encounters and conversations he has had with practitioners, performers and scholars of theatre.

In the Preface to the book, Barba sets out the principal questions that he has long done battle with and that will form the cargo that the canoe will carry on its journey; the questions are:

What is the performer's presence? Why, when two performers execute the same actions, is one believable and the other not? Is talent also a technique? Can a performer who does not move hold the spectator's attention? Of what does energy in the theatre consist? Is there such a thing as pre-expressive work?

(1995: ix)

As readers of the book, we are invited to create our own dialogue with Barba, share our reflections and experiences. Do not, Barba warns, accept at face value what is written; question the ideas and the practice, and look beneath the surface.

The first chapter does not begin in the theatre. As ever with Barba, we are asked to take several steps backwards in order to see the picture better. We begin with what Barba calls the 'culture of faith'. This idea, he says, is recalled first through his senses, and it concerns his catholic upbringing, living with his grandmother in Gallipoli, southern Italy. He recounts a story of seeing his grandmother combing her long hair in a mirror, wearing a long white nightgown, from one angle she appeared as a young bride, from another angle she appeared as an old woman. This image he calls, 'The moment of truth when opposites embrace each other' (1995: 2). You may recall from Chapter 1 that Barba says that we all need to find our own 'moment of truth'.

There is a strong similarity between the image of the grandmother in Barba's story and a character called Doña Musica created by Julia Varley, who appears in both *Kaosmos* and *Doña Musica's Butterflies* (see Figures 2.1 and 2.2). Why does he evoke the image? One reading or interpretation may be because, as a metaphor, it captures an essential aspect of theatre anthropology. First, that we should not accept something at face value but look beneath the surface, second, it also draws on an opposition of youth and old age and opposition is a principle of the pre-expressive. (We will return to this notion of the pre-expressive later in this chapter.) Barba continues to tell his story, and explains that at 14 when he went to military school he was struck

**Figure 2.1** Julia Varley as Doña Musica in *Doña Musica's Butterflies*.
Photograph by Jan Rüsz

**Figure 2.2** Julia Varley as Doña Musica in *Kaosmos* with Jan Ferslev.
Photograph by Jan Rüsz

by the way that the civic ceremony, for example the parades and marching, unlike the sacred ceremony in the Catholic Church, was only concerned with outward appearance. As a soldier you are expected to respond to orders and perform actions at a surface level, without thought or emotional response. The 'culture of faith', as he calls his experience with religion, on the contrary, involved the whole body, both physically and mentally. The military he describes as the 'culture of corrosion' as it cancels out thought and feeling, splitting them off and privileging action. Barba uses the example of immobility to illustrate the difference between the 'culture of faith' and the 'culture of corrosion'. He states that immobility in prayer demands the projection of the whole self, both body and mind, towards one thing (an invisible mobility and mental activity), whereas the immobility of the soldier standing to attention demands a physical immobility and a mental stagnation. From the 'culture of corrosion' Barba takes us to the 'culture of revolt'. Leaving Italy at 17 he rejected family and culture, desiring instead the experience of being foreign. In Norway, as an immigrant who did not speak the language he was forced to read communication through facial expression and gestures, as he could not understand the spoken language. Barba developed the ability to decipher people's attitude through the smallest perceptible impulse in their behaviour. You may recall how similar this idea is to the teachings of Meyerhold and Stanislavsky, referred to in Chapter 1. They observed that the smallest perceptible action in a performer's behaviour communicates something to someone else. The 'culture of revolt', then, reveals the way in which Barba has reflected on his own experience in relation to theatre practice that he has researched and learnt from, and formulated the experience as a key principle of theatre anthropology.

## AN IMPULSE TO ACT DIFFERENTLY

According to Barba, the practitioners Stanislavsky, Brecht, Meyerhold, Artaud, Grotowski and Copeau have all been heretics, rebels and reformers because they have all transformed theatre and created what he calls a theatre of transition. Barba says that we can only emulate them if we also live in a state of transition; '[t]ransition is itself a culture' (1995: 5). He insists that being in transition, like a floating island, has enabled him to make connections between one theatrical practice and another. He explains that although he has always been fascinated by Japanese, Balinese and Indian theatre, the long periods of spoken text in their performances have been daunting, as he does not understand the language. During the long periods of spoken text, Barba would focus on a detail of the performer's behaviour: their foot, their eyes or hands. From this close observation of their performance behaviour he came upon a coincidence: that Asian performers and the Odin performers worked with their knees slightly bent. You will see that in Chapter 4 we are required to maintain this position when doing exercises and creative work. At Odin they call this position the sats, an impulse towards action and the body being in a state of readiness for action. This position can also be seen as a basic position in sports activities; if we watch a tennis player about to receive a serve or a goalkeeper about to try to save a penalty we can see a complete state of readiness in their behaviour. The recognition of a common posture formed the first principle of theatre anthropology: that is, an alteration in balance that is different from our everyday balance; the balance is not one that we use or need in our everyday behaviour but an altered balance.

## IN PURSUIT OF CULTURAL PERFORMANCES

In 1978, for three months, the Odin actors separated and travelled to different places, such as Asia and South America, and learnt other styles of performing; for example, **Buyo** from Japan and **Legong** from Bali. This form of learning was not fully approved of by Barba who believed that learning with the intention of merely imitating another performer would only lead to a surface understanding rather than an embodied understanding. In such a short time the actors could not become expert practitioners of Legong or Buyo but they were able to acquire a different understanding of how the body might use energy and a different range of physical behaviours that were far removed from their everyday behaviour, what is referred to within theatre anthropology as extra-daily behaviour. The actors then used the experiences of working with these different physical behaviours in their own developing practice.

Barba wanted to know whether the similarities in behaviour that he had observed between his Odin actors and the Asian performances were common to other performance traditions, and what the principles were that underpinned the performance styles that, as spectators, we see. Thus it was that he held the first session of ISTA in 1980 in Germany. As Barba says, he does not claim to be an expert on all of these performance traditions from China, India, Japan and Bali, but he was, and is still, intrigued to uncover what might be below the surface of the characters, stories, costumes and make-up. He says that it has been through seeing Asian theatre and the work at Odin that he has been reunited with the 'culture of faith', a 'unity of the senses' (1995: 7) that he first found in the rituals and ceremonies of the Catholic Church. The first chapter, then, fills in the picture of how theatre anthropology was first conceived.

## DEFINITIONS AND PRINCIPLES

The opening statement to chapter two gives us a clear and concise definition of theatre anthropology. It says: 'Theatre Anthropology is the study of the pre-expressive scenic behaviour upon which different genres, styles, roles, and personal or collective traditions are all based' (Barba, 1995: 9).

By 'theatre', Barba refers inclusively to both theatre and dance. Barba also uses the terms North Pole and South Pole to separate different types of performance behaviour. However, he is aware that any form of categorisation is fraught with problems, for example, terms such as East and West are problematic as they exclude many peoples of the world and create artificially constructed borders. East and West politically have represented a hierarchical position where the West has been considered to be superior to the East. North Pole and South Pole also suggest artificial borders, although Barba would argue that the terms have an equal status. By 'North Pole', Barba refers to performers from a codified performance tradition, for example ballet, Kathakali and Noh theatre, and 'South Pole' refers to performers with no codified tradition, for example, most modern European theatre would be an example of this. (See Barba's chapter three, 'Recurring Principles', for more on this subject.) Whether a performer is 'North Pole' or 'South Pole', theatre anthropology is concerned with the principles that performers use to transform from their daily selves. These principles engage both the mind and body and exist at the level of technique: 'If there is physical training, there must also be mental training' (Barba, 1985: 370). What is not being studied by theatre anthropology is the application of the techniques in a performance context.

The second chapter cites the terms that theatre anthropology has identified to describe or explain these principles, for example, **scenic bios**, theatrically **decided**, pre-expressive. Although initially alien, these terms are concrete ones that aim to reveal what it is to be an actor. Barba argues that the field of study and the terms also enable the actor to be more reflective and aware of what it is to learn. Whatever the tradition, and there are numerous traditions that are all substantially different on the surface, when we embark on a process of learning there are key principles that we learn first. As stated in Chapter 1, we learn to walk, sit, stand, express attitudes and emotions using facial expression and hands. All of these things are learnt in daily life, that is inculturated, but we learn them again for theatre, through a process of acculturation. Barba has noted that there are common principles underlying all genres and styles of performance and these are the foundations from which we each begin to build our theatre tradition. It is only by leaving our familiar territory behind and encountering those different traditions that we can better understand what it is that we do, and recognise that there are similarities as well as differences.

## ENERGY AND LIFE IN THEATRE

'Theatre anthropology is a study *of* the performer and *for* the performer' (1995: 13). Its first task, says Barba, is to trace the recurring principles identified in diverse theatre traditions, not to homogenise them, that is make them all the same, or distil them down to a set of predetermined rules for performing, but to identify what different strategies performers use to create actions and energy. One of these recurring principles explores the paradoxical use of energy in life and in theatre. In life we have succeeded in using the least amount of energy in our daily behaviour; we often slouch when we sit, stand or walk. In theatre we need to expend the most amount of energy, 'dilate' the body as Barba says. Doing everyday activities both with and without energy helps us to understand the term 'scenic bios', the quality of live-ness that the actor needs to communicate something. Try some everyday activities (for example, watching, listening, looking, waiting) first with the least amount of energy and then dilating the energy. Dilating the energy does not necessarily mean that you do the action 100 times bigger or faster: it means that you engage the whole body in the activity and focus all the energy on the activity, and this includes both physical and mental energy. The whole body should be committed to making the action real and not illustration or pantomime. On reflecting how the exercise works, you may recollect and make links with the experience of doing the boxing exercise in Chapter 1.

It is the quality of mental energy, or mental dilation, that distinguishes the virtuosity of a performer. To be virtuosic is to show great skill or technique: for example, an acrobat uses their body to amaze the spectator, whereas the actor uses their body to inform the spectator (1995: 16). The ability to use energy effectively as an actor is also referred to as the scenic presence of the actor; that is, what the performer must do to attract the attention of the spectator in performance. Altering your balance from an everyday balance, and dilating the body, creates a transformation in the body, making it 'hot' or 'extra-daily', and is the first step to activating your energy. (For more information on 'dilation' see Barba and Savarese, 1991: 54.)

## THE PRINCIPLE OF ALTERATION IN BALANCE

Considering our shape, it is a feat of engineering that enables us to stand up straight and to remain balanced. We only have our feet in contact with the ground and so even the smallest change in that contact can throw the body out of balance. But these changes can also bring for the performer a dynamic energy, which emphasises or draws attention to our live-ness in the performance space. A distortion in balance is clearly evident in codified performance traditions, for example, in classical ballet where the dancer is obliged to learn the first position, second and third, how to plié, work on point, etc. All of these positions and moves demand a distortion of the body's natural balance. However, it is not only in codified forms of performance that the performer utilises this principle: Billy Connolly, a stand-up comedian, and Dario Fo, the Italian writer and actor, also evidence this precariousness of balance when performing on the stage. It is not always evident to the spectator that balance is being played with in this artificial manner, as the play is not necessarily about an exaggeration of visible action. Often the play of balance is veiled from the spectator by the elaborate costumes that the actor is wearing. It is important to note that it is the effect or consequence of the imbalance that creates a quality of energy in the actor that attracts the spectator's attention (see Figure 2.3). By bringing together many different examples of performance practice and different

**Figure 2.3** Iben Nagel Rasmussen in action during the work demonstration *Whispering Winds*. Photograph by Tony D'Urso

voices of performers describing how and what they were taught, Barba illustrates the numerous ways in which balance has been played with. He provides examples of work you might do to experience a different, 'extra-daily' balance. For example, try some simple ways of altering your balance by walking using only the outsides of your feet, or the inside edge of your foot, or with the big toe raised. Remember to do the exercises in bare feet and keep your knees soft and check on what adjustments you need to make to your body to effectively walk in these different ways: what happens to your hips, your spine, your arms? Try to keep the walk going for as long as possible so that you can get used to the new balance and reflect on its effect on your body.

## THE PRINCIPLE OF OPPOSITION

A second principle observed by Barba in the different traditions he has encountered is the 'principle of opposition', which he says all performers use 'consciously or unconsciously' (1995: 24). Unconsciously, we follow this principle automatically. Anatomically, the body necessitates that, in order not to fall over, a counter balance is always found: for example, to counter the body's weight going forward a leg must go out to support the body and find a new point of balance. Barba has observed how this physical necessity has been refined in art. Many performance practices work with precarious balance as a technique, as it requires the performer to dilate their energy and be 'scenically alive'. For example, working on point in ballet, the ballerina needs to make the movements look light, graceful and effortless, whereas she actually needs to be working extremely hard to hold her balance and create this illusion. Look at the examples cited in the *Dictionary of Theatre Anthropology* and try to adopt the stances illustrated (see pages 176–185). Hold the position for as long as you can to understand how you have needed to change your balance and where all the oppositions are in the position. Then try to move, adjusting the oppositions with each move that you make. Take the exercise slowly and try to attain fluid movements (see Figure 2.4).

## THE PRINCIPLE OF 'CONSISTENT INCONSISTENCY'

The third principle of the pre-expressive is that of 'incoherent coherence' (see Barba, 1985) or, as it is referred to in *The Paper Canoe*,

**Figure 2.4** Julia Varley demonstrating the idea of oppositions during the work demonstration *The Dead Brother*. Photograph by Tony D'Urso

'consistent inconsistency'. This is where behaviour is inconsistent or incoherent with everyday behaviour but is coherent or consistent within the realm of the theatrical practice. This principle operates beyond mere stylistic differences and artificial behaviours and, again, involves a quality of energy and thinking that is consistent and believable to the spectator. As part of the process of developing a performance behaviour that is consistent but not a part of their everyday behaviour, the performer needs to use the idea of omission. Omission in this context means leaving out certain parts of an action or simplifying a movement. In the *Dictionary of Theatre Anthropology* omission is explained as being like a comic strip where each frame contains the minimum but essential information to make sense of the story. There are gaps and leaps between each comic frame that, as readers, we make sense of as being a part of the style. In a similar way we understand and can identify the characteristics and devices that are used in theatre and, in particular, in the actor's craft. We need to identify what characteristics our particular theatre will have. If we were a solo performer telling the story of, for example, 'Little Red Riding Hood', with no set and only a minimum of costume and props, we would need to decide how we were going to create all the different characters and spaces that the story demands, and make the story clear for the audience. To perform every moment in the story may be too laborious, so we have to omit, refine and condense the story and the performance down to their essentials. Another example of omission cited in the dictionary is that of 'performing absence' (Barba and Savarese, 1991: 174). Stage-hands are sometimes in view of the audience but we treat them as invisible or absent. As an actor we might not leave the stage space but we might need to indicate that we are no longer a part of the fiction. We need to create conventions that can be understood by the audience that indicate what is, and what is not, a part of the fiction. The idea of omission is complex, but arose from the shared experiences identified by many different performers from different performance traditions when trying to explain the skill of trying to condense or intensify an action into a smaller space but with the same intensity. The process of omission can be achieved by taking out extraneous actions, reducing an action in size but not in intensity or focusing on opposition and resistance in one part of the body. These are all approaches that are used by different performers, as you can see in the examples cited in the dictionary. As Barba says, the beauty of omission is 'the life which is revealed with a maximum of intensity and a minimum of activity' (1995: 29). The actor who is able to dance on the inside while appearing to be completely immobile on the outside demonstrates a good example of omission. Omission should not be confused with an actor who, when required to reduce an action in space, just makes the action with one hand while the rest of the body is dormant and without energy. Rather, it is about reducing the action without losing any of the intensity, and engaging the *whole* body. As an actor it is possible to draw the spectator's attention to certain parts of the body, but this is achieved by using the whole body. Try the following exercise to experience stillness on the outside but movement on the inside. Working alone, move freely around in the space, as though waltzing with a partner. On the command 'freeze', immediately stop but allow the momentum and feeling of the movement to continue inside of you for as long as possible. As soon as the physical sensation fades, or you become mentally distracted, begin to 'dance' around the space again. Each time you freeze the action try to hold it for longer.

## THE PRINCIPLE OF EQUIVALENCE

Another term that Barba introduces in this chapter is equivalence. It is equivalence, Barba argues, that distinguishes art from everyday behaviour. Equivalence is contained, he says, in the idea of something that is both indicating the past and suggesting the future. Again, the notion of opposition is brought into play, as Barba recounts an example from the mime practitioner Etienne **Decroux**, who showed that to reproduce daily life in mime the opposite physical movement needed to be done. To give the illusion of pulling a very heavy object the actor needed to find an equivalent physical action. This could be achieved by using an imaginary resistance of pushing a very heavy object. Barba adds that an action on the stage must be real but it is not important that it be realistic (1995: 32). Try the mime of pushing as an exercise to explore the way in which opposite forces work in the body. Begin by pushing either against a partner or a wall, with one leg in front of the other so that you can feel what it is like, noting where the forces are in the body. For example, energy is exerted in the back leg, chest and arms; the spine and front leg are soft. Keeping the same intensity of effort, do the same action alone, or away from the wall. Without the resistance we are likely to fall over so we need to find an equivalent way of using energy, or exertion, that will enable us to show the action of pushing. Observe how, in the transition from working with a partner or wall to working alone, your weight will shift from your back leg to your front leg and your spine will actively arch and become strong, while your chest becomes soft. The shifts in weight, balance and energy required by the performer to give the illusion of a pushing action are subtle but important to observe and perform with precision.

We need to be able to represent not what we are but what we want to show: thus, equivalence indicates both the past and the future. This process may entail breaking down what we do in life and rebuilding equivalents to this behaviour for the purposes of creating believable performances, which communicate to the spectator. We need to be able to break away from the conventional behaviour patterns we have in life and look in detail at what it is that we want to communicate and how that might be achieved. Different traditions have very different strategies, and certainly the codified traditions like ballet, Kathakali, Beijing Opera have formalised a very different performance language from the languages of everyday life. Barba stresses that we need to go beyond merely resembling ourselves as a human body in performance.

## THE PRINCIPLE OF THE 'DECIDED BODY'

The final term that Barba introduces in chapter three is that of the 'decided body'. The term 'decided' is not to be understood literally as an actor being in the process of deciding or carrying out the action of deciding. Barba points out that language does not translate the full implications of the term: it is only through experience that we can fully grasp what it means. However, although the term can only be fully comprehended through experience, Barba provides images and associations that help us to get nearer to the term. He suggests that it is achieved when an actor is immersed in the theatrical reality that is their tradition to the point where the artificiality is experienced as normal behaviour within that space; the work no longer needs to be mentally considered or translated by the mind for the body – usefully, mind and body are working as one.

## TO RECAP

At the end of the chapter Barba usefully recaps on the main principles of theatre anthropology that have been identified through the research undertaken by ISTA. These are the principles identified as the pre-expressive:

- alteration in balance;
- law of opposition;
- consistent inconsistency.

These principles are components or levels of organisation of the actor's scenic bios, that is, the actor's presence, the way in which he or she can be identified as scenically alive and attract the attention of the spectator. The principles lead towards the actor being able to dilate his/her energy, both physically and mentally: dilation in turn enables her/him to perform at an extra-daily level necessary for theatre. The extra-daily behaviour of the actor entails breaking with everyday behaviours and finding equivalents. Equivalence is the opposite of imitation: it reproduces reality by means of another system, a fiction but a fiction rooted in real actions.

As a final point in this chapter Barba suggests that whatever tradition an actor comes from, whether it be a Stanislavsky tradition or a Kathakali tradition, what the performer is looking for is a '*fictive body*, not a fictive person' (1995: 35). By fictive body, Barba is reminding us that we are not only performing when the character we are representing is specifically involved in the dramatic narrative, we also fulfil many other functions in our fictive state. Noh and Kabuki actors illustrate the point, although the drama has finished, they retain the fictive body and move slowly off stage. They are not themselves and they are not the character that they have been representing but they continue to perform the logic of the fictional world (see Barba and Savarese, 1991: 195).

## QUESTIONS AND CRITICISMS

Chapter four is made up of short responses and ideas about theatre anthropology. It does not need to be read in a linear fashion but can be dipped into, although each section does in some way follow on from the previous note. Each section is like a part of a montage, in that it can be read individually or as a part of the whole chapter. Each note can be considered as an invitation to begin a dialogue with the author, or an opportunity to pause and reflect on the many issues that he raises here. Barba engages us in discussions of technique, anonymity, theatre as the art of the spectator, theatre anthropology as the premise of ethics, and the thorny question of whether theatre anthropology can be considered a science. 'Notes for the Perplexed' does not set out to resolve all of these questions and it does not seek to cure the problem of being perplexed, if anything it highlights being perplexed as being an active and constructive state. The notes give responses to many of the criticisms that have been aimed at theatre anthropology. For example, some critics have questioned why Barba has focused mainly on Asian theatre practices when he argues that the principles underlie all performance practice. Does he privilege North Pole, or codified theatre, over South Pole, or non-codified theatre? Other criticism has called into question the use of scientific language that is sometimes used and has asked whether theatre anthropology proposes itself as scientifically objective? Certainly, scholars and academics from the fields of anthropology and theatre have questioned whether theatre anthropology is the most appropriate term for the research (see De Marinis, 1995; Munk, 1986; Zarrilli, 1988).

We may feel no less perplexed at the end of the chapter, but, as Barba says at the beginning of the chapter, '[w]e can leave as a legacy to others that which we ourselves have not wholly consumed' (1995: 36). As performers, spectators, directors of theatre we engage with many questions regarding such issues as: who is theatre for? Are there common principles of performance? How does a performer engage the attention of the spectator? Many of these questions have been handed down as legacies from previous eras and, in turn, we may continue to hand them down to generations following us. In this chapter Barba invites us to engage in the debates that have, and continue to perplex him.

## ENERGY OR, RATHER, THE THOUGHT

Chapter five returns to the knotty concept of the performer and energy. The word 'energy' cannot be avoided, says Barba, and performers often translate it falsely: thinking it means making actions bigger or more exaggerated. Surely, if a performance is energetic enough the spectators will be impressed. This is to misunderstand what makes an effective performance. As Barba says, bombarding the spectator with energy in the form of loud voices, a furious pace and exaggerated gestures does not engage, but alienate (1995: 51). The performer's task is to focus and model energy. The actor must 'use subtlety, feints and counterfeints. Only in rare, carefully planned cases is a powerful action effective' (ibid.). Again, using anecdotes from his own experience and experiences from other practitioners, Barba tries to show us what it is to learn and comprehend. He uses examples from Stanislavsky, Meyerhold, the Russian film-maker Sergei **Eisenstein**, and the German maker of dance theatre Pina **Bausch** to illustrate the condensation or miniaturising of the energy of an action. He reports that Pina Bausch said that it is important for the dancer to be able 'to dance in the body before dancing with the body' (1995: 54). The emphasis here is on that which is invisible to the spectator, the internal dance or the internal score of the actor. If the body is dilated but the mind is not, effective communication with the spectator cannot take place. We can learn the moves and actions and reproduce them, but without the creative engagement of the head the performance will be dull; the performer is not present in the moment. The point takes us back to Barba's experience at military school and the 'culture of corrosion' (1995: 3), a state whereby we accept and imitate precisely, but with the body alone.

As part of the discussion on energy, Barba explores the concept of 'sats' in relation to similar terms used by Meyerhold (pre-acting), Grotowski (pre-movement) and Decroux (immobile immobility). All of these terms attempt to define the moment of preparation by the body before an action, and the shift of emphasis or direction in preparation for the next action. This procedure is not staccato in effect but should flow smoothly while clearly marking each new sats, each new small change in energy. As actors we do not want to draw attention to these moments; this would anticipate the action so the spectator could see what we were about to do before we did it. It is a part of our invisible preparation. What the spectator should receive is a sense of energy that is always ready to act or react, always in the moment. Some people might refer to the sats as the impulse for an action. When learning any technique, whether it is the piano or driving a car we need to begin slowly and mechanistically, going through the process, or order of actions, so that each element can be identified and performed precisely. By artificially slowing down an action we can identify where an action begins to be performed in the body and where it is pre-formed, that is, identifying what prior preparation is necessary for the action to take place. Again, we must be wary of thinking that sats, as an impulse, begins as a thought process; that thought precedes action. Sats unites thought and action and is experienced as both working as one. Barba recounts an example of a performer from Beijing Opera who, describing a sequence of performance, used the phrase 'Movement stop, inside no stop'. This, said Barba, inadvertently defined the 'value' of sats to a performer (1995: 58). It is also an alternative way of thinking about omission (see the waltzing exercise on page 55). Return to the waltzing exercise and repeat it: imagine that you are gracefully waltzing around the space with a partner and on the command 'freeze', immediately stop moving, but allow the movement to continue on the inside. As you do the exercise be reflective: be aware of how the experiences of the actions affect your energy and focus. When you are still, allow the physical momentum and thought or image to carry on in the body for as long as possible before you move off again.

As you will probably have begun to notice, there are some aspects of theatre anthropology that appear to be very similar to each other and there is often overlap between them; for example, equivalence contains opposition and alteration of balance. This is because the terms are often being used to mark a small but important part of the process of acting. A single sequence will employ physical and mental dilation, scenic bios, scenic presence, and many examples of alteration of balance, the law of oppositions, consistent inconsistency, omission, resistance, being decided and sats. It is like learning the grammatical construction of language: once we are familiar with the many parts, we are able to use them creatively to communicate our own ideas, moods and actions and develop our own particular style. Observe a partner performing a sequence of actions and list as many of the different principles from theatre anthropology that you can see the performer using.

Still focusing on the quality of energy, Barba goes on to introduce two terms derived from the discipline of psychology: **anima** and **animus**. Anima-energy is defined as soft and delicate and animus-energy is defined as vigorous and strong (1995: 60). Barba is quick to point out that the terms should not be read in relation to masculine and feminine energy; this, he says, would be misleading and unhelpful. The body in performance, says Barba, is an 'art body', a 'non-natural body'. Barba says that we should think of ourselves as neither male nor female. The body 'has the sex it has chosen to represent' (1995: 62). To prejudge what constitutes the attributes of femaleness or maleness in a character is to reduce the exploration and potential of what, as an actor, we might and can do. In performance, characters are made of many characteristics. To be selective and reduce the possible characteristics to either masculine or feminine is lazy. Anima and animus are terms used to describe the quality of energy needed to express an action (physical or vocal). Actions may be inflected, emphasised or modulated differently to create different effects. It is only through the experience of playing with actions that we can discover the potential energy, whether animus and/or anima; again, it is not something that we should anticipate. The terms should also not be seen as polarities; an either/or. As a model, anima and animus serve to mark the extreme points of expression through energy as though on a continuum, through work we can discover the 'gamut of nuances which lie between them' (1995: 67).

## 'PATHS OF THOUGHT'

Barba moves on to explore the concept of energy and the notion of sats in relation to the Japanese concept of *jo–ha–kyu*. *Jo-ha-kyu* is described as 'a criteria – or paths of thought – which in Japan regulate the arts' (1995: 69). The structure of *jo-ha-kyu* is cyclical, similar to sats; where one action stops, another begins. In the action of ending one action is the action of beginning the next. The three parts of the structure are called resistance, rupture and acceleration. The complexity of the Japanese performer's score is revealed in Barba's description of the process of continually subdividing each part of the *jo-ha-kyu* into smaller and smaller sub-divisions of an action. This process could, in theory, go on into infinity. Although this extreme of the process is not necessarily useful in itself, it does give the performer a very particular rhythm of thinking. Although it appears that their performance of a particular Noh character is precisely the same as their teacher's, there will be subtle differences in their use of improvised rhythms and energy. These subtle but significant differences are barely perceptible to the spectator but give the performance the quality of being performed for the first time, its scenic bios. To illustrate how the three phases of *jo-ha-kyu* can be identified, return again to the waltzing exercise. The first phase – *jo* – is described as resistance and could be applied to the first moments of the waltz, where the performer is physically establishing the imaginary resistance that would be created by a dance partner as they begin to move around the space. The second phase – *ha* – is described as a rupture of the resistance and an increase in the motion. As the action of waltzing develops and becomes more fluid so the momentum can be increased without losing either focus or intensity and this could be identified as 'ha'. The third phase – *kyu* – is described as a sudden stop. The moment of 'stop', as Barba says, is a transitional phase: 'the movement is interrupted but the energy is suspended' (1995: 69) and becomes a point of departure for a new *jo*. This moment can be identified as the 'freeze' in the waltz exercise. Having sub-divided the waltz exercise into three initial component parts we could go on to sub-divide the *jo* section into a further *jo-ha-kyu*, and so on. You might try to see how far you can divide up each phase of the exercise. Perhaps one of the most problematic aspects of the pre-expressive to understand, in practice, is how performers might construct a drama-turgy by artificially reshaping energy, and transforming their natural bios into scenic bios (1995: 71). Barba says that as a performer we need to think of energy in

> tangible, visible, audible forms, must picture it, divide it into a scale, withhold it, suspend it in an immobility which acts, guide it with varying intensities and velocities, through the design of movements, as if through a slalom course.
>
> (1995: 71)

For these patterns or 'designs of movements' to be transformed from the pre-expressive level, to the level of dramaturgical composition required for performance (a score), the performer needs to allow for 'voluntary disorientation' (1995: 87). We need to relinquish our usual concern with establishing what the work might mean, what Barba calls 'fetishism for meaning' (ibid.) and also resist the need to work only for results. We need to be able to play. To further illustrate this idea of how creative work can be generated, Barba refers us to the book *The Sleepwalkers* by Arthur **Koestler** and the idea Koestler refers to as a creative '**pre-condition**'. Barba employs this idea to explain the relationship between the body and the mind when we are working creatively. Koestler describes the 'creative pre-condition' as a moment before a creative act is achieved where we regress to a more primitive, but creative, level of being. We might understand this level as being the state we achieve through exercise and play where the social, emotional and physical barriers that we have constructed to protect ourselves in our everyday life are overcome. Barba believes, from the work that he has done with actors, that this seeming state of chaos, or primitive regression, is essential to the production of creative work and, rather than avoiding or evading it, we should enjoy and revel in it. Barba talks about energy and creative thought working in leaps that constantly change in direction and that rather than trying to tame them we should allow them full rein. These leaps, he describes using the Aristotelian term '**peripeteia**'. In tragedy, peripeteia describes the moment when one action causes another to develop in an unexpected way, so causing a surprise for the spectator. Barba is emphatic that as performers we need to find ways of surprising ourselves when we are working creatively and warns that this will not happen if we are always working for results.

The chapter concludes with what appears to be rather odd advice from Barba after the perilous canoe journey he has taken us on. Having travelled way back in history and to some of the furthest points on the globe, we are brought back to Europe and the last century. He tells us to read Michael **Chekhov**'s manual for the actor *To the Actor*, subtitled *On the Technique of Acting*, published in 1953. 'It is one of the best actor's manuals. It should be read and reread, reflected upon, pried into', says Barba (1995: 73). By citing exercises from Chekhov's manual and including quotations from Stanislavsky and Meyerhold we might ask, as Barba does, why we have needed to travel so far from home? He responds by answering that 'only the length of the voyage makes it possible for us to discover the riches of home upon our return' (1995: 80). In addition, we can sometimes only make new discoveries and find new understandings in the work we do at home by approaching it from a different perspective or in relation to other experiences that we have had. Barba and Odin never advocate taking the shortest and easiest route between A and B because this will not enable us to make discoveries, enrich our experiences and make the most interesting work.

## LEAPS OF THOUGHT AND A SEARCH FOR MEANING

Chapter six, like chapter four, is again made up of a series of notes and is subtitled 'Notes on the Search for Meaning'. The chapter begins with a story from Barba's life in Poland and his visits to Berlin to see Brecht's theatre. It depicts Europe in ruins, the 'spirit of the times', and asks how do we make theatre that means something, that resists the museum and the 'spirit of the times'? He tells us the story of Antigone, drawing parallels between Antigone's defiant act of scattering earth on the body of her dead but unburied brother, and theatre, as both being 'empty and ineffective rituals' (1995: 85). Both Antigone's act and theatre are, and need to be, driven by personal necessity, argues Barba, not, as we noted in Chapter 1, by audience taste or the 'spirit of the times'.

Barba goes on to tell tales of spectators at a Kathakali performance who sleep, chatter, eat and appear indifferent to the performance. The Kathakali performers, says Barba, have humility because they understand that their performance serves the story that they tell. The audience have come to see not them but the characters and stories that they are representing.

The story of Captain Van der Decken and his ship *The Flying Dutchman* serves to illustrate the way in which unexpected changes, peripeteias, or leaps of thought can take place. The story tells of a captain battling with his ship on the stormy seas. He curses God and proclaims that he will not be defeated 'until the last day'. God's retort is to condemn the captain and his ship to be forever at sea. This story has been mutated and inverted in the many versions of the story that have been created. The versions of the story have been borne from 'leaps of thought' from those that have been touched or inspired by their own experiences in relation to the captain's story. Barba remarks that, '*The Flying Dutchman* is exemplary. The leaps of thought . . . ought to be characteristic of the behaviour of the "collective mind" of the ensemble working on a performance' (1995: 91).

Some of the notes or stories revolve around the problems of meaning for theatre. Barba comments that when making theatre we often get caught up with trying to predetermine meaning, to collectively agree on what a performance will mean before we begin rehearsing rather than allowing meanings to emerge from the play of ideas. He observes that a theatre company do not have to agree on the meaning of what they do as they will draw meaning from the images and associations that are personal to each of them. A director who tries to impose coherence and a rational meaning on a production before the process of rehearsal has begun curtails the actor's creativity, which could lead to shallow and one-dimensional work. We have to be prepared to take risks with our work, says Barba, and abandon our need for results and meaning.

Other stories in the chapter draw on science and sociological studies. One tells of children's drawings and how they reflect a child's experience of the world but work according to a single logic that, as adults, we might consider to be innocent or naive. Adult drawings may appear to be more sophisticated, again often working according to a single logic, but one that is accepted as normative, or standard, within that society. The point that Barba is making is that in his opinion 'good art' consists of more than one approach to logic. A composition using multiple logics allows for both the normative rules of a tradition and personal experience to be reflected in a work of art. The theatre has the advantage of being able to reflect numerous logics within the same space at the same time, allowing the spectator to select and weave their own logical meaning from the phantasms that float in front of them. Patrice Pavis, a theatre semiotician and a member of the scientific staff at several ISTA meetings, has described the experience of seeing an Odin performance as being like a dream where many images and parts of images drift past us in sleep and when awake we try to order them and make logical connections and meanings from them. We will return to Pavis in the following chapter on performances.

Further into the chapter Barba recounts anecdotes about the theatre practitioner Decroux and the Indian **Odissi** dancer Sanjukta Panigrahi, with whom he worked very closely and co-founded ISTA. He tells us an enigmatic tale of his dream to transmit the knowledge of building a Trellaborg, a Danish term for a fortress without walls that traps and tames the winds from the ocean. The legend of Trella tells of a princess who was prevented from safely landing on the shores of Denmark by the winds. When at last she was able to land, way off her desired course, she built a fortress to harness the winds, and was then able to travel on her way. He says that his theatre is a Trellaborg.

Last, he gives an account of being at a performance in Italy with Grotowski, watching work that Barba describes ironically as 'Grotowskian' because it used candles, something that Grotowski never did. It is a poignant story filled with anger and frustration that this was not an example of the 'freedom in theatre' (1995: 100) that he and Grotowski had been fighting for. This performance was being held as some sort of homage to Grotowski. Barba recounts that, although it aspired to be a ritual, it was no more than an empty ritual; it was as dead as a museum piece.

The chapter meanders and travels across troubled water, at times we appear to be lost or disoriented but we need to remember that these are 'notes on a search for meaning' and Barba carries us, by way of these notes, not to meaning but what he describes as 'a fistful of water'. Like the water slipping through our fingers, meaning too is elusive. We think we have it and in an instant it has escaped. Often we miss or neglect the experience offered by a performance, imagining that there must be one essential meaning that needs to be grasped. Perhaps the lesson for the spectator is that we should allow ourselves to be immersed in the water, be affected by it and reflect on how it has affected us, rather than standing on the edges keeping dry. At the end of the 'closed' session (for invited participants only) of ISTA in Umeå, Barba gathered all the participants in a room and announced that he was going to give us all a gift. All he asked was that we accept the gift and then leave the room without disclosing the nature of the gift with anyone else. Each of us made our way to him, shook his hand and then we were each asked to put our hand into an ornate metal container covered with an ornate rug, take out our gift and then leave. I put my hand in the bowl and pulled out a handful of snow. Clutching the snow to me I left the room and then sat and reflected on the gift I had been given. Initially, the snow was hard and cold, freezing against my skin. Slowly, as it began to melt it turned into water and slipped away through my fingers, and the sensation became one of burning. Both the snow and I had been transformed, and the meaning of the gift was embedded in the experience. The gift was a metaphor and encapsulated many of the principles of theatre anthropology.

## BUILDING OUR OWN THEATRE

Theatre cannot solely be defined in terms of a fixed structure or building but by the form of the actor's body. But can the form of the actor's body be fixed?

In chapter seven, Barba most clearly reveals another aspect of his wealth of knowledge regarding theatre. Barba is not only a theatre practitioner committed to making theatre and researching the craft of the performer but he is also a theatre historian. The opening account in the chapter describes a Congress meeting in 1934 in Italy, held to discuss the plight of theatre and questioning whether a new design for theatre architecture was what was required to make theatre effective and meaningful. Many notable names from European theatre contributed to the congress and Barba draws our attention to the notion proposed by Edward Gordon Craig, which stated that it was not the architectural construction of the theatre that should be our concern but the actor whose body 'embodies an architecture in motion: a Form' (1995: 102). This 'Form', Barba compares to the 'performer's pre-expressive level of organisation' (1995: 104). The congress serves to illustrate that the questions asked by Barba are questions that have continued to perplex theatre practitioners, actors, designers and directors through history. Essentially, the product of the performer's work is ephemeral. Attempts to fix, for example, the role of *Hamlet* so that every aspect of the role is always played in exactly the same way, with the same moves and the same intonation of the text, is to go against the nature of performer and performance. While **Laban**'s schema for notating movement aids the performer in fixing and replicating the form of choreographic movement, other practitioners have attempted to go even further and record every aspect of a production: the costumes, design, relationship of music to gesture, etc. so that the form of the production could be exactly repeated at any time by any company. What these methods of fixing form have shown is that they can only ever be partially successful because what lies at the centre of performance is the living form of the performer. As Barba has advised us before, we need to take several steps back from where we think the problem is to begin work. It is not the structure or the content of the work that needs to be fixed but the pre-expressive form of the actor.

Two particular criticisms have been levelled at the research into the pre-expressive; the first being that separating the performance, or the expressive level, from the preparatory level is impossible and, second, that whatever a performer performs in front of a spectator will be read as having meaning. Neither of these criticisms is denied by Barba but he does counter them by saying that it is possible to select and observe certain features of a performer's work and place the observations in a particular context for the purposes of research. Importantly, spectators at ISTA need to consider themselves to be observers looking at process and not finished product. As Barba says, we can choose to behave like any other empirical researcher who selects an area of research and treats it *as if* it was autonomous; to establish operatively useful limits, to concentrate on these limits and to make an inventory of them; to compare, find and specify certain functional logics; and then to reconnect that field to the whole from which it was separated for cognitive purposes only.

(1995: 105)

Although this approach sounds scientific and is, indeed, adopted by scientists (Barba refers to the ISTA academics as 'scientific staff'), he is not claiming that the work is scientifically proven. What he is interested in, and wants to share, is the value of observing and questioning performance behaviour in a very particular context, namely theatre anthropology. Indeed, in 1988, a session was organised by the Centre for Performance Research, titled 'Theatre, anthropology and theatre anthropology', to discuss the relationships between the different disciplines of anthropology, theatre and this new area of theatre anthropology. Historically, scientists from areas that might be considered 'hard sciences', like physics or chemistry, have not accepted anthropology as a legitimate science. Anthropologists have been required to defend their discipline, and its right to be considered a science. In turn, many anthropologists would question whether theatre anthropology can be a legitimate branch of anthropology; they would certainly question it as having a basis in science. Categorising and naming has always been a contentious arena. Perhaps now, more than ever before, there has been a blurring of boundaries between traditionally exclusive areas of science, high art and popular culture. When Grotowski changed the name of his theatre in Opole to a laboratory, there followed a great deal of confusion and debate as to what a theatre laboratory might be. Defining our own use of terms is, perhaps, what is most important, and Barba is clear what he intends by theatre anthropology. That this definition has changed over the years is a consequence of the research, questions, debates and criticisms that have arisen from inside of, and outside of, the ISTA sessions (the first definition is in Barba, 1986a, 'Theatre Anthropology: The First Hypothesis'; the definition was clarified in his retort to Zarrilli in Barba, 1988b; and in 1991 the definition changed again in *A Dictionary of Theatre Anthropology*; the latest definition is in *The Paper Canoe*).

The ISTA 'laboratory' is not looking to find a cure for theatrical malaise, or a formula for scenic presence. Indeed, it is notable that ISTA is not called a laboratory, but a school. Barba refutes the criticism that

ISTA follows a pedagogical paradigm but is a school where there is an 'open association of individuals who are each other's students and teachers' (Barba, 1988b: 8). The aim is to explore ideas of process before they become product. By process Barba intends that ISTA participants should explore the different levels of organisation that constitute pre-expressive theatrical behaviour: scenic bios, energy, presence (see Figure 2.5). These levels of organisation are not independent of expression and performance behaviour but can be observed separately. They can be useful but only, and Barba is emphatic on this point, in relation to the body and behaviour of the theatrical performer, '*in a situation of organised representation*' (1995: 108). Previously it was noted that there were some similarities with the training work and performance undertaken by athletes, but their work is not the same as an actor's and cannot be defined in terms of the pre-expressive. Although there is a case that an athlete uses sats, alteration of balance and opposition in an extra-daily manner, the intention is not to represent, communicate or inform, but to compete.

The 'design of movements', the 'pattern of movements' are terms Barba references to describe exercises. Exercises are learnt and repeated but only very rarely do they make the transition from being a part of training to performance for others. For this to effectively occur the exercise needs to shift from being a technical or creative challenge for the performer to being 'real' for the spectator. The use of exercises in an actor's training serves not only to introduce her/him to a specific form of theatre but, with perseverance, exercises will give her/him an independence to develop within a style individually. As noted before, we use exercises like bricks to build our own theatre, the exercises may be the same but the result can be very different. What Barba's chapter is striving to emphasise is a theatre building does not pre-empt the theatre that will take place within its walls, neither should the performer pre-empt what they can and will do. Although exercises are an integral part of the actor's training, they do not in themselves constitute a performance but, like the bricks, they give the actor a framework of possibilities. The paradox for the actor is that they work in a fictional and artificial context but their actions must be real. As Barba says, it is easy to be realistic and difficult to carry out real actions. Whether the work the actor does comes from the practices of Brecht or Stanislavsky, Barba shows that it begins at the pre-expressive level.

**Figure 2.5** Kanichi Hanayagi teaching a class during a 'closed' session at ISTA, 2000. Photograph by Fiora Bemporad

Apart from illustrating his argument that the pre-expressive principles are fundamental principles of the actor's craft, Barba, in this chapter, gives us an insight into how both Brecht and Stanislavsky worked with actors. He demonstrates how, although their ideas appear polarised, there are many overlaps and agreements in their two approaches. Barba also notes that Grotowski followed far more in Stanislavsky's footsteps than it may at first appear.

The canoe journey in this chapter appears to be around a pond rather than intrepidly across oceans. Time and again we drift off only to find that we have come back to the principles of the pre-expressive. Barba invites us to sort through the baggage that has been accumulated from the practitioners and practices encountered on the canoe journey and select what is most useful and necessary, not just to our understanding of theatre anthropology but also to our own theatre practice. We are encouraged to join up our thinking and observe the similarities and differences between theatre practices. For instance, Meyerhold encouraged his actors to apply different logic to different aspects of the performance score: the feet may be strong and military-like, while the hands may be soft and gentle, and the voice is seductive. Similarly, in many Asian forms of theatre, Kathakali for example, different parts of the body use energy, rhythm and pace differently within a single sequence of action. The eyes may be soft and seductive while the hands are working with a hard and vigorous energy and the feet may be creating yet another opposition by being gentle but hesitant. (We will be exploring the idea of working with different and opposing logic in the exercises in Chapter 4.) Barba points out that, in his later work, Stanislavsky no longer began a rehearsal process with actors using the playwright's text, but chose instead to extract an outline of actions from the play. He would then work with individual actors by delving ever deeper into the sub-divided micro-actions of the text. Thus, each actor created their own score before meeting up with the other actors' scores and the playwright's score. This approach to a score, Stanislavsky believed, freed the performance text from obvious and literal interpretation. It is an approach taken further by Meyerhold and developed upon by Barba and the Odin actors in their work on subscore. There are also notable similarities with the Japanese approach of *jo-ha-kyu*. The score, like Laban's notation, fixes the form, it is the 'theatre not made of bricks and stones' (1995: 130). Ryszard Cieslak, an actor with

Grotowski, recounts how his score enabled him each night to perform the work afresh, every detail of the score had been worked through over the months of rehearsals so that he was fully prepared for each performance: 'The score remains the same, but everything is different because I am different' (in Barba, 1995: 130).

## 'CANOES, BUTTERFLIES AND A HORSE'

Avoid expressing yourselves with metaphors when dealing with a pedant! He takes everything literally and then torments you.

(Meyerhold in Barba, 1995: 138)

Although Barba and the Odin actors have been at pains to transmit their experiences through workshops and practical work demonstrations, they are also dependent on the written word to convey their experiences. We often give the written word more of our time and respect than our bodies and actual theatre practice. Too often we distrust our bodies and our ability to communicate without words and transform experience into embodied knowledge. Perhaps this is because training is a very lonely task and demands great fortitude and determination. Perhaps words appear to give us stronger footholds to pull ourselves up, than the mystical secrets of performance experience, which can often appear unfathomable. Being able to watch a process and translate it into physical action is an important skill. Barba requires actors to be able to watch in the sense of observing and understanding behaviour and action at an embodied level: 'to see with the spirit is to grasp the substance; to see with the eyes is merely to observe the effect' (in Barba and Savarese, 1991: 244).

Barba reminds us that 'terminology is taken from practice' (Stanislavsky in Barba, 1995: 139) but he feels the need, in this final chapter of *The Paper Canoe*, to clarify how words are being used. The words in the book have already been through many forms of translation. The words have come from the practice that was observed and recorded in fragments of notes written on paper. These papers eventually built the 'canoe' for Barba's book. In addition, *The Paper Canoe* is translated from Barba's Italian, and my chapter is a version of what Barba says, and so we are drifting further and further away from the thing itself: the practical research that is theatre anthropology.

The final pages of the book bring us back to the practice, in the form of an account of a week of practical work, led by Barba, with a group of dancers and choreographers. The account describes the daily tasks that he set for them, the comments and advice that he gave them on where they might focus in the work, and what hazards to watch out for in the work. On their final day, in his final comments to the dancers, he emphasises the point that: '[y]our extra-daily technique must remain your point of departure. You must invent a dramaturgy of your own in order to weave the actions in sequences while conserving their back-bones and melting the metal of technique' (1995: 172).

In an earlier article, 'The Dilated Body', Barba tells us: 'An actor who draws only upon what he already knows involuntarily immerses himself in a stagnant pool, using his energy in a repetitive way' (1985: 370). We will return to the series of exercises that Barba recounts here and put some of them into practice as a way of accessing the principles of theatre anthropology from our own points of departure.

*The Paper Canoe* is not fixated on looking for results but, rather, processes in the form of the pre-expressive. The following chapter will begin to explore the transition of the process into performance. As a guide to theatre anthropology, *The Paper Canoe* enables us to peer behind the stage curtain and scrutinise the performer's creative process. Not only does it provide us with a guide to the craft of acting but it also gives us an insight into theatre practices from different cultures and encourages us to revisit and reread European practitioners from the twentieth century. The inclusion of such a diverse range of theatre practitioners and practices is not to suggest a homogenised theatricality, one whereby either everything is boiled down to the same thing or where each example is made to conform to the principles of theatre anthropology. Barba celebrates the differences but is also fascinated by the similarities and commonalities that exist beneath the surface of what the actor does. Although a reader might want to take this guide as a theory, Barba constantly encourages us to make our own way, try out exercises, and reflect on what we find. We should test out the terms and see how they might be of use to us. An anecdote in the 'Notes for the Perplexed' tells of an actress who scornfully rejects the book as arid; she asks what good it can be to her? Barba replies that it provides channels and reservoirs but she, as the actor, must provide the water.

## A FINAL THOUGHT

For Barba, a key question has always been 'how are you doing this?'. He tells a story about being in India and, having travelled for weeks in a car, arriving in a town where there was to be a live concert. The concert was extraordinary and he asks the performers, 'how are you doing this?'. The performers reply, 'but it has taken us fifty years to reach here and you want us to tell you in a few sentences!'. As Barba reminds us, the question is always the first day (Barba, 1999c).

# 3

# A SPECTATOR'S VIEW
## OF *EGO FAUST*

Barba has directed over 20 productions with the Odin Teatret and the Theatrum Mundi Ensemble. The performance we are going to specifically explore is *Ego Faust* (available on video from Odin Teatret Film) performed at the XII session of ISTA held in Germany in 2000 by the Theatrum Mundi Ensemble. The ensemble is a transient company made up from the artistic staff, musicians and Odin actors attending the ISTA session. At the end of the session the ensemble present a performance as a gift or barter for the local community who have hosted the school. A Theatrum Mundi performance has been performed at the close of most of the 12 ISTA sessions. The form and content, while remaining similar, have progressively been refined and further developed with each performance.

In the previous chapter we explored theatre anthropology and the recurring principles used by performers at, what Barba calls, the pre-expressive level of organisation. We are now going to explore the way Barba creates a performance and how we as spectators might find levels of readability, or meaning, in the work. *Ego Faust*, like the other ISTA performances, differs from the Odin performances because the dramaturgy is not as complex or as complete. This is because the performance at ISTA is constructed in a matter of days, rather than Odin performances, like *Mythos* and *Kaosmos*, which are worked on for many months. However, the ISTA performance is particularly interesting because it contains elements of practice derived from ISTA research and demonstrates some aspects of Odin's approach to performance. *Ego Faust*, despite only having been worked on for a few days, does illustrate a complex dramaturgy because it has been developed over the 12 previous ISTA sessions; however, it remains incomplete.

The storyline, on which Barba's *Ego Faust* is based, is derived from two main sources, one by the English playwright Christopher **Marlowe** and the second by the German writer Johann Wolfgang von **Goethe**. Both the stories tell of a man, Doctor Faustus or Faust, a philosopher and scientist who, bored with his lifetime of academic study, uses his knowledge to conjure up an evil spirit. The spirit comes to him in the form of the devil's servant Mephistopheles. In return for Mephistopheles working to increase Faust's knowledge and power, Faust signs a pact selling his soul to the devil when he dies.

## SYNOPSIS OF THE *EGO FAUST* PERFORMANCE

In order to follow the analysis of *Ego Faust* you will need to imagine, from the details that follow, that you are a spectator at the performance. The stage has been erected outside a large public building and an auditorium for the spectators has been specially erected for the occasion. The first event that takes place involves a young girl running down the central aisle of the auditorium, up some steps, onto the stage, crying 'mama', and into the arms of a woman. The woman, who stands at the front of the stage, rejects the girl and throws her to the ground. Both figures are wearing contemporary western dress. This event is set apart from the theatricality of the rest of the performance: it is lit differently and the clothing is everyday. We need to carefully consider why it is there, and its implications, at a later stage in our analysis. Our attention is then directed to a level above the stage. A spotlight picks out an elderly male figure dressed in a dressing gown. He directly addresses the audience in Italian. We become aware, from what he says, that this figure is the central character of Faust. Two figures emerge onto the stage into a pool of light. One figure is male and dressed in top hat and tailcoat and the other figure is female, dressed in a long black coat and hat with a veil shrouding her face. The two figures meet on the stage and slowly dance around each other; there is a mixture of eerie musical and vocal sounds accompanying them in their strange dance. Faust enters onto the stage followed closely by a huge, grotesque figure, with a skull for a head and wearing evening dress; this is an Odin figure named Mr Peanut, created and performed by Julia Varley. The Mr Peanut figure, we are told in the programme, represents 'Death'. Death is accompanied by a masked figure in a richly coloured costume; the programme tells us this is 'Old Age' further research shows that this figure comes from the Balinese tradition of **Topeng** and the character is called Tua or 'old man'. The figure of Faust appears to be oblivious to the presence of these two figures. Slowly, as all the figures move about the stage, drapes covering the back of the stage are raised up to reveal the splendid façade of an actual building, various musicians and other performers. Faust, addressing the audience, introduces the two figures in black as Mephistopheles. Other colourful figures enter the space: a Balinese clown, a Balinese assistant to the witch **Rangda** known in Bali as **Pangpang** and another Balinese figure, the **Garuda** bird.

The male Mephistopheles tempts Faust by showing him what he desires; in this instance beautiful young women. Faust can have everything he wishes if he signs over his soul to the devil. The female Mephistopheles pulls a quill from her hat for Faust to sign the pact and, with only a slight hesitation, Faust signs. As he signs, the male Mephistopheles holds Faust's hand and the tip of the quill is forced through the paper and into his hand like a dagger. The music breaks into upbeat rhythms and as the party begins Faust is in agony. We then see Faust being rejuvenated: the dressing gown is removed to reveal a very smart evening dress suit and the shabby grey hair is replaced by smartly groomed hair. Faust's whole demeanour becomes more agile and youthful. Hovering behind him, like a shadow, is the figure of Mr Peanut representing Death, who is also dressed in a version of Faust's evening dress. The figure of Death hovers behind Faust throughout the performance. Faust is presented with a bell that will grant him whatever he wishes. The beautiful women are led away by Rangda, the witch figure from Bali. Research indicates (see Bandem and deBoer, 1995) that Rangda is reputed to gather together young women at night in the graveyard, corrupt them and teach them the dark arts, and turn them into witches. The suggestion here might be that these beautiful young women shown to Faust may not be what they seem. Faust calls for entertainment and he and Mephistopheles go and sit with the audience. Two grotesque Balinese clowns enter with a large sign announcing the presentation of 'The Tragedy of Gonzalez' by 'The Royal Danish Players'. This is a reference to the dumb show and play-within-a-play from *Hamlet*. Indeed, we see the same scenario enacted. We see a young queen with her elderly husband dancing together formally, until he feebly lies on the ground to sleep. The queen takes the opportunity to poison him, he dies and she fakes her grieving until another, younger man enters. At this point she removes her black widow's clothing to reveal a seductive, silver and scarlet gown and they dance a tantalising dance together (see Figure 3.1). His dance is similar to that of 'the foreign king', a villain from the Balinese **Gambuh** and her dance is derived from the Spanish Flamenco. Faust has learnt nothing from the pantomime performed for him and goes in search of a beautiful woman among the audience. He soon finds his ideal, his 'Helen' as she is named in Marlowe's version of the Faust myth; here she is named Margherita. It is Goethe's version of the story that is being enacted here as Margherita parallels his character of Gretchen, a shortened form of the name Margherita. The character of Gretchen was based on a woman known to Goethe named Susanna Margherita Brandt, who was executed in 1772 for killing her illegitimate baby. As we will see, as the story unfolds, it is by no accident that the character is named Margherita. The role here is performed by an **onnagata**, that is, a male performer who, in Japanese Kabuki, specialises in female impersonation. The female role, as performed by the onnagata, is considered to be a feminine ideal; she is graceful, delicate, submissive and demure. This woman, Margherita, entrances Faust and waits on his every need. Behind Margherita and Faust, the figures of Death and other demons playfully mock the lovers' scene and, in the background, the female Mephistopheles sings a beautiful-sounding song. In a solo spotlight the male Mephistopheles enters and conjures two young girls to play. Faust is distracted from his love-making with Margherita by the girls, suggesting that he might move on to seduce them. Margherita tries to persuade him to stay with her until eventually he rejects her, pushing her to the ground. Death has taken on the form of a bride, wearing a white veil and garland of dead flowers on the skull head, and takes Margherita to one side. Death gives her something wrapped in a cloth; we are invited to read this as a baby from the way the bundle is held. Margherita lays the small bundle on the ground and, with great anguish, takes up a stone and strikes the bundle and then makes as if to bury it.

**Figure 3.1** Roberta Carreri and I Nyoman Budi Artha in 'The Tragedy of Gonzalez' in *Ego Faust*. Photograph by Fiora Bemporad

A peasant woman appears scattering seed and planting out rice. Faust goes from one woman to another and then decides to ring his bell at the peasant woman. She attends him and he lies with his head in her lap as they tease each other playfully. Margherita looks on and there is a great confusion of characters in the space, many different voices singing and music playing. Margherita is distraught and is being shadowed by Death, still dressed as a bride. The programme informs us that there are three performers on stage who all play Mad Margherita. The three Mad Margheritas, Margherita, and a variety of demons, dance in confusion around the stage with a cacophony of music accompanying them. The confusion of figures, movements and sounds indicates that Margherita has been driven to distraction, having submitted to Faust's seduction and then killed her illegitimate child. An important element of the onnagata's performance is his skill in transforming his costume on stage, as though by magic. The costume change occurs at this point of high dramatic tension and Margherita, now all in white, sails off through the audience. Although we might not know whether this is a typical moment in Kabuki, and what the sign means, we have enough information to read Margherita's exit as her death. Mephistopheles and Faust find the bundle of cloth. Wrapped inside the cloth is a child's shirt. The shirt is stuffed into the mouth of the Garuda bird, also known as the bird-of-ill-omen, who carries it away.

There is now a change in scene, pace and dynamic, indicated by two performers creating a banqueting table, by holding a long piece of white cloth on the stage. Faust enters and appears to sit at the table. Various comic characters from different cultural traditions enter and perform for Faust's entertainment. From the audience a Japanese figure appears, perhaps the ghost of Margherita, or an avenging demon (see Figure 3.2). Two additional Japanese male warrior figures enter and enact a sword fight. **Shishi**, a Japanese lion figure, **Barong**, a Balinese animal figure, Mr Peanut as the figure of Death and the Balinese witch figure, Rangda, all enter, followed by various other figures. The music builds and chaos and confusion envelops the stage. Amid the chaos and confusion, Faust is de-robed and dressed in female attire. His behaviour

**Figure 3.2** Kanichi Hanayagi and Sae Nanaogi performing at ISTA, 2000.
Photograph by Fiora Bemporad

becomes wild and demented. The drapes covering the back of the stage are lowered, as red glowing smoke rises from behind the building into the night sky. All the characters leave the stage through a central doorway in the façade of the building, into the red glow. This we understand to represent Hell. The peasant woman and Mr Peanut as Death remain and he begins to transform into a woman, who then nurses the skull-head and torso, dressed like Faust in an evening jacket. Julia Varley, who created and plays Mr Peanut, carries the puppet-like skull and torso and this moment of separation is skilfully and theatrically achieved. The peasant woman continues with her everyday work, quietly singing. As she sees the remains of Mr Peanut (or perhaps it is now Faust) in the woman's arms, she begins to grieve and takes the figure into her own arms. A child's voice is heard calling 'mama' and a young girl appears running down the centre aisle, up onto the stage, into the arms of the woman (also played by Julia Varley). The woman rejects the girl, pushes her to the ground, takes her belt and beats the child. The performance ends.

During my description of *Ego Faust* you may have noticed that some of my comments have been informed by my understanding of theatre from different cultures. By contextualising the work we begin to find our way through the experience. To further develop our understanding of the performance we need to find an appropriate and useful form of analysis to apply to the performance. Analysis will help us to unpack and reveal the many associations, details and possible meanings available in the performance.

## PURPOSE OF ANALYSIS

There are many different ways in which we might analyse a theatre performance. Analysis is not an end in itself but enables us to develop an understanding or reading of a theatre performance, both as a creative act and in terms of meaning(s). The analytic method we use, or the questions that we ask, will be determined by the sort of information we want to find out. An analysis can only ever give us a partial reading of a performance, in that it will only provide us with a framework to the questions that the analysis poses. The analytic framework that we will apply in this chapter is based on a model devised by the French semiotician Patrice Pavis (2003). What is particularly useful about Pavis's model is that it combines four stages, each of which asks particular questions and gives us substantial information, that when combined work towards giving us a reading of the production. One of the first questions we need to ask ourselves is, 'what is the purpose of the analysis?'. Is the intention that it should serve us as a spectator or as a maker of theatre? If we are working from the position of a spectator we may begin with a descriptive analysis. Descriptive analysis requires us to look at the content: characters, props, costumes, set, actions, music, speech, in fact all those aspects that contribute to our understanding of what happens in the performance. At a basic level, a descriptive analysis will enable us to identify whether there is a narrative and what that narrative might be. When we develop the descriptive analysis further to look, beyond narrative, at the possible meanings being generated in a performance, we interpret what we see, hear and experience in relation to who we are and what we know. Interpretation raises the complex issue of plurality; this means that there can be many different readings of a single performance, each of which can be equally valid.

If we are analysing a performance from the perspective of a theatre-maker then we may be more interested in structural analysis: not *what* happens but *how* it happens. For example, we might look at whether there are patterns, themes, motives or other structural devices being used in the performance and how they relate to each other to give a coherent structure to the performance. This structural approach can give us more fixed or concrete information. The four stages in Pavis's model combine both descriptive and structural readings along with a final stage where the information from the previous three stages is brought together to give us what he calls an 'ideological' reading. In addition, theatre anthropology offers us another way of developing a reading of performance work, in terms of the pre-expressive. Theatre anthropology gives us insights into the structural aspects of a performance and we will use our understanding of it in our analysis of the performance. Pavis's analytic method has been constructed with Odin and ISTA's work in mind and certainly levels 1 and 3 are derived from ideas drawn from theatre anthropology.

As we have already noted from the previous chapter, Barba discusses some of the problems inherent in searching for meaning and explanation in theatre, in chapter six of *The Paper Canoe*. From what he writes, we know that we need to approach their theatre work from a different perspective from one which we might be familiar with for traditional, narrative structured plays, from the European theatre tradition. For one thing, the experience that is stimulated for us by a performance may be far more important than a search for meaning or explanation. Barba suggests that as spectators we tend to try to predetermine meaning rather than allowing meanings to emerge from the play of ideas and associations that a performance might offer. It may be useful to see Barba's theatre work on a kind of continuum where we might have, for example, a soap opera from television at one end and, at the other end, the experience of sitting watching people go about their business in a market. The soap opera is structured to have several story lines running at the same time in an episode, some may be concluding, others may be being introduced, while others may be reaching a climax. If we are familiar with the soap opera and the characters, then we will be used to the process of reading across the various stories and will not be concerned when, at the end of the episode, we do not know what the conclusion to all the stories might be. At the other end of our continuum, we have the market place, where there are lots of people coming and going who we do not know, each has their own particular intention, which we also do not know, only the space and activity gives us a sense of structure and time. Barba's work falls nearer to the market place end of the continuum.

## INITIAL RESPONSE

As with any analysis, we should begin by recording our first impressions of a performance. My first impression of the *Ego Faust* performance was similar to the experience I had when I first saw Odin Teatret perform a piece called *Anabasis* in Wales when I was 18. Although I did not know what was going on, I was deeply affected by the performance. Initially, I found both performances to be chaotic, loud, colourful, confusing, sometimes funny and sometimes very haunting. I noticed that they referenced or included different cultural practices but I did not know what these were. It is a typical feature of Odin and Theatrum Mundi performances that they use little spoken language and often when they do speak it is not in English. The actors are encouraged to use their native language when speaking in a performance. As Barba has said, the aim is to create a 'theatre that dances'. Both *Anabasis* and *Ego Faust* have used a great deal of song and dance, but much of it was unfamiliar to me. Although the performances were vibrant, colourful and included wonderful and delightful characters, I sometimes felt excluded because I did not know who or what they were; this sometimes left me feeling bored and disaffected. In *Anabasis* I thought that there might be a narrative driving what happened in the performance and became anxious that I was not able to understand it. When I gave up trying to find a narrative I discovered that I was able to create my own and that this was far more fun. In *Ego Faust*, I was aware that there were interesting juxtapositions being made between the different cultures represented in the performance but I did not know why this might be, whether it was intentional, or significant, or whether it was successful. Structurally, I noticed that there were moments in both performances of high activity followed by quiet solo moments. The use of music was often unexpected in relation to what was happening in the performance. Despite my confusion, many of the images from the *Anabasis* performance have stayed with me and have continued to inspire, delight and intrigue me. I have seen two versions of the Theatrum Mundi performance, and the video version numerous times, and still find the experience enchanting and fascinating.

## QUESTIONS WE MIGHT ASK

Having recorded our first impressions we now need to draw up a list of questions from these impressions that will help us to better understand the performances and develop an analysis of the work. The questions may be different if we are starting from the point of view of a spectator rather than a theatre-maker. Here is a list of possible questions we might begin by asking from the point of view of a spectator:

- What is happening?
- Who are the characters being represented and why have they been selected?
- What does the title of the performance mean?
- The performance works as spectacle but is it theatre?
- Why do they use so much music and dance?
- What music, songs and dances are being used?
- Is the selection significant?
- What do the different cultural references mean?
- Why do they interweave so many different cultural references?

- Were some moments in the performance unsatisfactory because I did not understand them or was this problem to do with the composition of the performance?
- Does the performance have a narrative structure or is it structured in a fragmentary manner from lots of images, like a montage?
- With the performance of *Ego Faust*, I could recognise some sections as being a part of the Faust story but other sections were unfamiliar and I did not understand them, so were they from another story or version of Faust?
- What function did the music play?
- Did the music enhance a sense of disruption and fragmentation in the performance?
- Was the performance coherent and if so how was it?

In addition to the above questions, these are questions that we might ask from a structural point of view:

- Is there a pattern in the way in which the scenes are structured?
- Are sounds connected to particular characters or figures: **leit-motiv**?
- Is there a relationship between the pattern of dance moves and the music being played?
- Is there a relationship between the chords and harmonies we hear and the action and number of performers in the space?
- Is the music being used as an adhesive, sticking the performance together, or is it being used to heighten the disjunctive relationship between what we hear and see?
- How are time and space established in the performance?
- Are there patterns in the spatial relationships of the performers on the stage?
- Does the performance set out to create an example of **inter-cultural** theatre and if so what does it tell us about the classification of intercultural performance?

The questions that have been posed here have arisen from my first impressions of the performance. Having drawn up a list of questions from our first impressions, the next stage is to see what answers we can fill in without doing any further research. In this instance, the title *Ego Faust* suggests that the performance is based on the well-known

European story of *Faust*. The term **Ego** comes from the Latin for 'I' and can also be found in the work of the psychoanalyst Sigmund **Freud**. Freud uses the term 'Ego' to define the conscious part of our personality that we show to the world. At this stage it is not clear why the two words have been put together so we might need to read the story of *Faust*, and undertake some research into Freud's ideas on personality, to look for possible connections. The performance runs for just over an hour and does not have an interval. There is no formal narrator figure in the performance telling the story, but the character of Faust does directly address the audience in a similar way to a narrator. The performance does not use blackouts to indicate a change of scene or place. The performance runs continuously and any changes to the direction of the story, or shifts in mood, are indicated by the actors and musicians. Scenes involving several performers and a fast pace are often followed by a change to the pace and a scene involving one or two performers. Time and place are not established as being fixed, suggesting that this is not an important question and that perhaps the performance aims to transcend both time and space. The programme gives us some information about who the characters are in *Ego Faust* but some of these characters are still unfamiliar. For example, Faust and Mephistopheles are both characters from the Faust story but who was Kleist's bear?

At this point it may be useful to introduce the Pavis model and overlay the questions on to the first three sections of his model.

## PAVIS'S MODEL

In his model Pavis describes a structure by which, he says, we are able to find a level of readability of the intercultural performance score. The structure incorporates four levels that are laid out as follows:

| CONDENSATION | DISPLACEMENT |
|---|---|
| (Accumulators) | (Connectors) |
| *(1) Formal readability* | *(2) Narrative readability* |
| Linear progression | Images progress conjunctively |
| Accumulation of forms, techniques that are condensed and filtered. | Images explicitly connected. |

| (Shifters) | (Secators) |
|---|---|
| *(4) Ideological readability* | *(3) Anti-narrative readability* |
| Performance can be read | Ruptures in linear progression |
| despite previous disruptions to | Montage |
| consensual ideology: a meeting | Disjunctive relationship of |
| or recognition. | signs due to theme, rhythm, |
| | geography |
| | Fragmented reading. |

(Pavis, 2003: 281)[1]

The four levels of readability that constitute the model are: (1) formal, (2) narrative, (3) anti-narrative and (4) ideological readability, or consensus.

Pavis's approach might be most clearly understood as a development of a **semiotic** analysis, that is the study of signs, but incorporating the principles of the pre-expressive from theatre anthropology. The spectator's aesthetic experience, or first impressions of the performance as spectacle, is important and should not be dismissed as unimportant but we need to recognise that this first level indicates a surface response to a sense of the beauty, delicacy or grotesqueness of a performance. Conversely, unless we undertake specific research into Japanese Kabuki theatre or Brazilian **Orixa** theatre, we are not going to be able to access the specific details of a performer's behaviour from those traditions.

## FIRST THOUGHTS ON PAVIS'S MODEL

In the model you will have noticed that Pavis uses two headings, **condensation** and **displacement**. Freud uses these two terms in his book *The Interpretation of Dreams* (1900). For the dreamer, like the artist, the dream or work of art is constructed from a series of associations, whereas for the critic or analyst, the process is to decode the event or dream by trying to retrace and unravel the associations. Due to the ephemerality of theatre work, the task for the analyst who

1   The Pavis model is derived from a draft English version, which was kindly sent to me by Pavis.

is a spectator is difficult but can be seen as a parallel to a person trying to retrieve their dream and make sense of it. The performance, once performed, cannot be returned to in its exact form, unlike a compact disc recording, a video, a novel or a sculpture. The dream stories are created from the dreamer's memory and it is here that representations can be abbreviated, translated or substituted. A significant aspect of this method of analysis is that both the actors and the spectators individually create a dream-like score to fix their experience and understanding of the performance.

## CONDENSATION

This part of the model explores the ways that we filter, edit-out and organise those aspects of a dream or performance that are unfamiliar. We condense the material into sequences that are logical and knowable to us. Pavis uses the term condensation in conjunction with 'formal readability' (1) and 'ideological readability' (4) on the diagram. As we will soon see, the first level, 'formal readability', involves accumulating fragments of material that have been selected by the actors for their score, that have then been combined by Barba and now represent the Theatrum Mundi Ensemble's particular performance practice. The composition of what is shown may draw from more than one tradition, as well as from unconnected parts of any single tradition. An example of this in *Ego Faust* is demonstrated during the play-within-a-play scene. Here, a Balinese performer plays the 'old king' using the Topeng figure of Tua. The queen, when seducing her new lover, dances in the Spanish Flamenco style and the new lover is a Balinese performer performing the 'foreign king' figure from the Gambuh tradition (see Figure 3.1).

If, at this stage, we were to try to encapsulate the whole performance by reducing it only to selected references that were familiar and made logical sense to us, we would be leaving out most of what was performed. The performance remains confusing because there are so many cultural references that are unfamiliar to us. By the final section of the model ('ideological readability': level 4) we are able to construct a reading of the performance from the accumulation of material that we have acquired from the previous levels of reading. The seemingly unconnected nature of the parts of the performance can be understood to reveal a sense or meaning, even if that meaning is that it does not have one single meaning. Using the example of *Ego Faust*, we will see that the performance is not a single dream but an ensemble of dreams that have already been filtered and re-dreamt by Barba before they reach the spectator. The spectator will then filter the accumulation of images and associations that he or she receives. However, each time the performance is received it is not only filtered but also elaborated upon. For example, in the game 'Chinese whispers', each time the phrase is passed on it is slightly changed. Similarly, when the performance or dream is filtered through someone's interpretation, it becomes elaborated and potentially more distorted. At some point, for example in the process of analysis, the event, or dream, will be verbally recounted and structured as a narrative. This is seen as the last distorting stage of the dream-work, or performance.

## DISPLACEMENT

Displacement occurs in Pavis's model in relation to connectors (narrative readability) and secators (anti-narrative readability). This part of the model explores the ways that we focus on an unfamiliar aspect of a performance and replace it with something familiar. What is evident in the dream, or in this case the performance space, may in actuality have been processed by both the actor and Barba, and developed on from the initial logic of an actor's individual physical and vocal score. The process of displacement enables the spectator, via the levels identified as 'narrative readability' (2), and 'anti-narrative readability' (3), to achieve a level of understanding, or readability, either based on similarity or proximity. This understanding is based on what was actually seen or experienced in the performance. In other words, what we as spectators see and experience, that appears as unconnected and unfamiliar, we displace or substitute with a series of our own associations and connections. These associations and connections give the performance a level of narrative readability that makes sense to us.

Of course, it can be misleading to reconstruct the experience of dreams in an intelligible and logical structure, as certain aspects of a dream will, by necessity, be ignored or repositioned to create a coherent logic. There will inevitably be a level of distortion. For each cultural group meanings are consensual, which means that we adopt particular behaviour and symbols and form an agreement on what they mean. These meanings are passed down from generation to generation. An example of an aspect of our culture that is consensual is the language we speak. It is important to note that meanings are not always reliant on language but can also be reliant on symbols, for example the image of a man being crucified is a symbol of the Christian religion. With the examples we are analysing we may recognise an aspect of the performance as symbolic but not know what it symbolically represents. For example, before the character of Margherita in *Ego Faust* exits she is transformed by the means of an extremely quick costume change on stage; we recognise this moment as significant but without detailed knowledge of how signs operate to give meaning in Japanese Kabuki theatre we can only guess at what the moment means.

The seemingly bizarre representations included in the performance of *Ego Faust* conjure up a fantasy that is both exotic and disturbing. Confronted with such fantastical and colourful figures the danger is that we as spectators suppress what they might represent in their cultural context and allow them to remain as strange, foreign and other. In the performance there is a dissociation of the object from its function so we do not only see a human being in the space behaving as a human being but also as a vessel for ideas and symbols, or a hieroglyph (a description Artaud gave to the performer after he had seen Balinese performers at the Colonial Exhibition, in Paris, in 1930). As a hieroglyph, the performer has the ability to explode our sense of ourselves. This is challenging, exciting and scary, a step into the unknown for most of us spectators who are used to watching actors only representing other human beings.

## LEVEL 1: FORMAL READABILITY (ACCUMULATORS)

At the first level of the model we are looking for clues in the performances given by the actors that will give us information concerning the way that they use energy and physicalise the narrative, and play a role or character in the performance. One way of assessing the kind of fictional world that is being represented is to look at how the actors behave in the performance space. In *Ego Faust* there is no theatrical set to give us clues as to where we are and so it is quickly apparent that where we are might not be important and that the focus of our attention should be on the actors/characters. In *Ego Faust* there is always a fracturing of the actor's body that has the effect of drawing the spectator's attention to a specific part of the performance space. As spectators of western theatrical traditions we are most familiar with the narrative coming from a spoken text, but in the example we are looking at there is very little spoken text so we need to look for clues in the physical gestures and actions used by the performers. Each of the actors in *Ego Faust* uses energy differently to construct different performance styles, and we can identify this by focusing on an aspect of their performance behaviour. For example, how they use their hands, facial expression and feet; also the dynamic of the movements gives us information that indicates mood, nuance or emotion. At this first level, as Pavis says, we accumulate the many forms of performance by isolating each one and follow the ways in which each performer uses energy, constructs role and narrative, physically and vocally. We then begin to organise the specific movement vocabulary used by an actor in order to identify how he or she constructs scenic presence. These events are processed sequentially and become part of the spectator's developing, cumulative understanding of the different performance styles presented in the performance. We then look for, and make connections across and between the different forms of, scenic presence to create our own reading of the performance. Level 1 investigates the performance from a structural perspective and does not consider the reading in relation to any narrative aspects. The reading that we develop at level 1 is fragmented but we recognise that the fragmentation is due to a lack of specific knowledge of the different cultural performance practices. Level 1 remains a partial reading as those aspects that we do not understand due to unfamiliarity, be it culturally, thematically or geographically, have yet to be explored.

Some of the information we identify as clues we might consider to be self-evident but what we need to be aware of is that it is we as readers of the performance who are sophisticated. We are able to read and formulate understandings about behaviour, both in life and theatre, at a high level because we are so used to interpreting signs in advertising, in films and on television. However, the danger inherent in our sophisticated reading is that we refute or dismiss the value of unfamiliar signs and view them as merely foreign and, therefore, odd. Within *Ego Faust* there is such a density of signs from different cultures that our job of decoding them is complicated. At level 1 we filter signs to just those that are familiar to us. We can see that a number of our questions fall into the first section of Pavis's model. Part of our confusion may arise from us not being able to identify or separate out the different performance styles so that the performance appears to be lots of people in colourful costumes rushing around at the same time. As an initial part of the process, Pavis suggests that the spectator makes a 'systematic fragmentary' observation of a performer, which would begin to open up the way in which the performer manages his or her energy, structures movement and, thus, is able to direct the spectator's gaze. For example, we might observe the male Mephistopheles, performed by the Brazilian Orixa performer, Augusto Omolú. Initially, his movements may appear strange to us but, by following him through the performance of *Ego Faust*, we can see that his actions are consistent in relation to everything else that he does. He has few spoken lines so his movements denote his character and the narrative that he tells. He moves fluidly from warrior-like movements, to seductive movements, to drunken movements. We are informed by the programme note that he plays the role of Mephistopheles but it is not a taking on of the character in a European sense: the way in which he has constructed his score is by assembling fragments from the many Orixa roles that exist into a score that depicts his responses and associations to the needs of the Faust narrative.

Augusto Omolú uses energy very differently to the Japanese performer, Kanichi Hanayagi, who plays Margherita, although again by following this performer we can identify that what the Japanese performer does is also coherent and consistent. It is as though each performer demonstrates an individual 'incoherent coherence' and that Barba, as the director, provides a framework or fictional space that, in turn, creates coherence to these seemingly different or incoherent theatre practices. The ability to shift the spectator's gaze from one part of the body to another is referred to as vectorising the body (Pavis, 2003: 125–127). Pavis's point is that the performer can perform in such a way as to draw attention to a particular part of their body, or that the analysis can focus on a particular vector of the performer's body and be able to draw conclusions about the way in which they use energy and create a character. By concentrating our attention on one fragment of a performer's body, a framework of analysis emerges that allows for a level of readability. We can see evidence of this in the Odin character of Mr Peanut. The performer inside the costume only has her hands visible to the audience as the giant puppet's skull head and torso that she carries hide her face. Her feet are also covered as she wears a long frock under the dress shirt and tailcoat worn by the puppet. However, although she can only communicate with her hands, she is skilfully able to suggest a range of emotions and behaviours in the character. It appears that the skull head is laughing, teasing, tormenting or flirting and this is a result of the actress being able to draw attention to a part of the body to communicate an action. By exploring the role of the peasant woman, who features for a short time in *Ego Faust*, we can observe how the energy of one performer contributes to our understanding of the performance. The noisy and often confusing mixing of characters and music that occurs in *Ego Faust* is offset by the consistency of the role of the character of a peasant woman, performed by Ni Wayan Sekarini, one of the Balinese troupe. When she first comes on stage she is cleaning, gathering and sowing rice. Occasionally, she crosses the performance space and sings as she scatters the rice, a symbol of the earth's replenishment and fecundity. Her actions are pedestrian, domestic, everyday but very closely observed. The action of scattering and cleaning the rice works as a counterpoint to the seemingly abstract physical codes, or codified vocabulary, used by the other performers and the simplicity and 'naturalness' of the activity becomes a strong focus in this otherwise elaborate spectacle. The world she inhabits is not filled with music; she is, in one sense, on the margins of the performance but she also represents a figure that celebrates, on a local level, human endeavour. In the same way in which we can look at the performers separately and identify their consistency of style and then re-evaluate the way in which the different performers work together, we can take the same approach with the musicians and identify that there is a particular rhythm and sound generated by the Brazilian drummers that is very different from the sounds of the Balinese **Gamelan**. Rather than hearing the mass of sounds as cacophonous, we can separate them out and then begin to hear them anew when they are playing together. What may have initially sounded and looked like a confusing and chaotic muddle of movements and sounds begins to exhibit a dialogue and patterns of harmonious communication existing between the disparate styles.

Pavis's first level of readability is described as 'formal' and reveals a structured and linear progression of what emerges as recognisable **signifiers** and **signified**, even though we may not comprehend what they might mean or represent. This level immediately highlights the way in which the example selected for analysis operates at the margins of western mainstream theatre practice as the performance uses signifiers that are not immediately apparent to a western spectator. The example has some recognisable elements but also includes many ambiguities. For example, in *Ego Faust* we learn from the programme that the character of Margherita is signified, or represented, by a Japanese performer who, in the performance, we identify as the character wearing a traditional Japanese dress, a Kimono, but the performer is male. Why is the main female character played by a male actor? Why are there two actors, one male and one female, playing Mephistopheles? Each example requires a certain level of interpretation and this initial level of the model can cause anxiety in us as spectators because of our desire to impose a coherent meaning by translating all the signifiers into recognisable material. A problem with this initial part of the process is that it can lead to a reduction and exclusion of material that does not fit a familiar, recognisable pattern. It is inevitable that as a consequence of the theatre that we have seen previously, we develop expectations. These expectations can cloud our judgement. We need to resist being bound by our cultural expectations and try to approach performances with an open mind and enjoy the play of possible meanings that we might identify in a performance. It is also important that we record the further questions that arise as we begin our analysis, as although some of these questions may be answered further on in our journey, many will inevitably demand specific research before they can be answered.

## LEVEL 2: NARRATIVE READABILITY (CONNECTORS)

The second level of readability covers building a narrative frame from the seemingly disparate fragments of the performance. We might understand this second level to be like a descriptive analysis. The narrative level is constructed by creating a reading from the connections that we can make between one moment and another. Another tool we might use here is the continuity of gestural signs used by a performer or character and how they relate to other actions in the performance space. For example, in *Ego Faust* we see a Balinese dancer wearing a costume with wings, she appears at intervals throughout the performance, she dances like a bird and is often given an article of clothing to carry away. We might read the connection between what she wears and how she behaves as representing what the programme names as Garuda, a bird-of-ill-omen. The significance of the clothing being taken away can be read, at a narrative level, as indicating death. This reading is supported by the repetition of her actions, which we can understand as a theatrical convention that denotes 'ill omen'. This convention is established early in the performance, although the spectator may not immediately understand the full significance of her actions. As spectators we try to make sense of what we see by forming connections between one moment and the next. This is, perhaps, the most difficult level to negotiate due to the fact that a characteristic of intercultural material can be that a performance does not always create a straightforward, developing narrative. Performances will often contain references and characters that are unfamiliar in our culture but are central to another culture's performance traditions.

There are some sections where it is evident that a story is being told in *Ego Faust* and further research will immediately help us to make appropriate and meaningful connections between these sections and other non-narrative, or challenging, moments. Finding out what the story of Faust is about is an essential starting point. As we read at the beginning of this chapter, *Ego Faust* is based on two versions of the Faust myth: that of Marlowe, in his English version dated between 1588 and 1593, and part of the story used by Goethe in his German version of the myth published in 1808. The account at the beginning of this chapter was composed in response to the descriptive level of Pavis's analysis. Initially, the account was very rudimentary and, although it gave a level of readability, it was generalised and would not have withstood close analytical scrutiny. For a more informed reading, the reader would need to undertake further research to discover why certain characters behave as they do, and whether certain actions have a particular significance within different cultural practices. An analysis of the relationship of the music to the performance is excluded at this level of the model, as, in many instances, it does not have a conjunctive relationship to the action. Pavis says that the materials used in a performance are constructed in a linear fashion that allows each piece to be seen as a separate moment. Observing and analysing these separate moments, he argues, allows for differences to be appreciated. Within this section of the analysis, Pavis suggests that Barba does not propose 'a reworking and a creolisation of traditional forms . . . dancers are being confronted with other traditions, improvising in their own style while being influenced by their "foreign" partners' (2003: 283). For example, in *Ego Faust* we see the Japanese onnagata performer improvising a scene of love and betrayal, derived from his repertoire of roles in Kabuki theatre, performing a dialogue with the Odin actor playing Faust (Torgeir Wethal), who is also improvising but drawing on information that he has developed as an Odin performer.

It may be useful at this point to consider the question of how an audience might view and interpret the complex dramaturgy of a performance such as *Ego Faust*, without the specialised knowledge that we have accumulated. Would an audience be able to see the performance as more than a spectacle of colourful and exotic cultural highlights? If this is not the case, then does that merely reaffirm the cultural differences as odd and strange? Although the intention may be to celebrate cultural differences is this what is achieved and if not is it a problem?

At the end of this second level of Pavis's model we have begun to resolve some of the questions that emerged from our first impressions. We have begun to construct a **fuzzy narrative**, a network of evident (or surface) narratives and narratives that are working below the surface narrative. We are clearer about why specific characters are involved in the performance, and what they represent. We understand that the interplay of different cultural performances has been selected for more than just an aesthetic reason. They contribute to the many levels of meaning that make the performance a richer experience, both at the level of surface narrative and deeper less evident narratives.

## LEVEL 3: ANTI-NARRATIVE READABILITY (SECATORS)

The third level of the model introduces the idea of anti-narrative aspects of readability (secators). We can tackle this level from both a structural and descriptive perspective. At this juncture, attention is focused on those aspects that either disrupt the idea of a linear narrative or the spectator's sense of familiarity with the material. Here, we are looking at those aspects that we previously left out, either because we did not understand them, or because they appeared not to fit the coherent descriptive and narrative level. The traditions, as was noted at the end of level 2, although disrupted and fragmented, always remain intact; they have not been fused together to create a hybrid but hold resolutely to their own sense of **proxemics** and **kinaesthetic** practices. The Theatrum Mundi Ensemble brings together performers from Bali, India, Japan, Brazil and the Odin Teatret. All of the performers have acculturated, or specifically learnt, performance techniques to contribute to the Theatrum Mundi work.

Let us now focus on some of the moments that remain unresolved following level 2. Pavis refers to these moments as ruptures and they are usually of a thematic, geographic or rhythmic type (Pavis, 2003: 281). In *Ego Faust* the musicians from India play while we see the Japanese onnagata performing stylised movements from the Kabuki tradition, this creates a rupture that is both geographic and rhythmic. These ruptures have the effect of dislocating the spectator's sense of time and space. Because the performance is not fixed in a time and space, we are invited to view the performance material **transcultur- ally**, that is, not historically or merely as exotic spectacle. Barba develops ruptures as a compositional strategy, exploiting the relationships between the performers, the musicians, as well as between performers and musicians. We might say that the geographic and rhythmic ruptures are central to the composition because the disjunctive relationships created between music and performance traditions invite the spectator to create and develop new ways of reading.

What has emerged from the theatre anthropology research at ISTA is that, while there are many differences in cultural performances on a surface level, there are fundamental similarities at a deeper level. We might liken the composition process to the way in which jazz music works. For example, a jazz musician is able to improvise at a surface level within predetermined harmonic structures. The Theatrum Mundi performers are also able to improvise, using material drawn from pre-existing structures that they have accumulated, or acculturated, as part of their cultural practice.

On first hearing music from the different cultures being performed simultaneously in *Ego Faust*, I could only hear a cacophony of sounds. As I became more familiar with the different musical textures, I was able to equate particular sounds with particular instruments and, subsequently, I began to hear the different musical traditions at work. As we look and listen more closely, and become more familiar with the performance, we can identify that, in fact, the rhythms are creating dialogues between the different performers, as well as the performers and musicians.

Earlier in the analysis, we raised the question, 'why is there a male and a female Mephistopheles?'. This question can now be explored as a thematic rupture because it breaks with the traditional convention of one actor playing one character. There is no obvious resolution to this question but one reading might be that Barba wanted to make an **intertextual** reference to another production of *Dr Faustus*, directed by Grotowski in 1963. Although not directly involved in the production, Barba saw and wrote about it in an article that is attributed to Grotowski (1964). In this production, Grotowski employed both a male and female Mephistopheles.

Another example of a thematic rupture concerns the presence of Kleist's bear at the banquet in *Ego Faust*. Initially, we might see the bear as another of the comic characters entertaining spectators in the auditorium, and Faust at the banquet. Who is Kleist's bear? Research reveals that Heinrich von Kleist wrote an essay called *On the Marionette Theatre* in 1810 and the essay contains the story of a bear. There is no direct connection between Kleist's essay and Faust, but several aspects of Kleist's essay provide some comment on themes found in the Faust myth. For example, both texts deal with themes such as, 'The Fall of Man' from innocence, as recorded in the book of Genesis in the Bible, human consciousness and the search for total knowledge. Faust signs away his soul to the devil in exchange for 24 years in which he wants to learn the secrets of life and death. Knowledge would give Faust power, perhaps the power of eternal life. With the power of eternal life, he would not need his soul. Faust has been described as a man who loves knowledge but hates learning. He consumes knowledge greedily but appears to learn nothing. He consumes the earthly pleasures of desire and lust but is not satisfied. For Faust, ultimate knowledge and pleasure remain elusive and the search for them leads to his demise. The paradox for Faust, and all other human beings, is highlighted in Kleist's essay. In the essay Kleist tells of a young man who is physically beautiful. One day he catches sight of himself in a mirror. He recognises how similar his image is to a much-acclaimed statue, renowned for representing masculine perfection. From that moment, the young man becomes obsessed with trying to recapture the moment when he first considered his own beauty. In his innocence he was beautiful but when he consciously became aware of himself, desire for perfection drove him further and further away from being able to achieve it. The essay continues with an account of a bear, which is able to deflect every thrust of a fencer's foil. The man fencing with the bear becomes more and more frustrated as the bear knows when an attack is real and when it is a feint, or mock. At the core of Kleist's essay is the idea that total knowledge can lead to harmony and completeness but that, paradoxically, being human means that we think, and to think means to have knowledge. Knowledge merely serves to remind us that there is always so much more to know. Therefore, we experience our selves as never knowing enough. We cannot be content with just being in the world because we are conscious of our past and our future – what we have had and what we want. The story of Kleist's bear is recounted by Barba in *The Paper Canoe* (pp. 60–61) and is used to illustrate sats, the premise being that understanding and knowledge come from experience, and being connected to the world: being in the moment and able to react.

The question of why the performance is titled *Ego Faust* finds a level of readability here at level 3. The human desire for pleasure that drives Faust is contained in Freud's term **Id.** Counter to the Id is the Ego, that part of us that is conscious, that rationally questions our desires. In life we experience a perpetual tension between the demands of the Id and the Ego. In Torgeir Wethal's performance of Faust we can physically see this tension in his physical actions and movements. There is a distinct difference between the movements of his head and the top part of his body, which remain thoughtful and more introvert, from the bottom part of his body, which is more dynamic and extrovert. The relationship identified here between Faust's desire for pleasure and his Ego indicates why the performance is called *Ego Faust*.

From a seemingly innocuous moment in *Ego Faust* we are now developing a significant network of communications. Another moment that is worth exploring in more depth occurs when Margherita's 'ghost' appears to Faust, towards the end of the performance. The culmination of this scene has Faust being led off into Hell. In Part 2 of Goethe's *Dr Faustus*, Margherita makes an appearance in the final scene of the play as 'The Penitent'. The scene takes place in the heavens and Faust's soul has been saved from the devil and is redeemed. 'The Penitent' asks that she might be his guide and the final lines of Goethe's epic drama tell us:

> All things corruptible
> Are but a parable;
> Earth's insufficiency
> Here finds fulfilment;
> Here the ineffable

Wins life through love;
Eternal Womanhood
Leads us above
(Goethe, 1959: Part 2, Act 5)

In a commentary on Goethe's play written by Walter Arndt (Goethe, 2001) these final lines are analysed; Arndt suggests that our will and desires, which are in opposition on earth, can be united through experience in Heaven, and allow us to finally achieve contentment. The dichotomy between our conscious rational self and our irrational self is transcended. As an additional note, it might be useful to remember that traditionally, in western thought (certainly since the philosopher Descartes said 'I think therefore I am', a statement that defined being human as primarily having to do with reason and thought, and not experience), the masculine has been equated with reason, knowledge and logic, and the feminine has been equated with the irrational, the emotional and experience. The union of the mind and body, or logic and experience, of the male and female is perhaps what brings us contentment. In *Ego Faust* we see Mephistopheles as both male and female and Mr Peanut dressed in male clothes on the upper body and female clothes on the lower body. In a similar way that the cultural, or geographic, ruptures open up dialogue between different cultural practices, so the gender ruptures open up dialogue between male and female.

In Barba's performance, Faust is not redeemed but he is stripped of his clothes and dressed in female attire (see Figures 3.3 and 3.4). As he becomes more and more demented he is eventually led off into Hell. We might read Faust's female clothing as referencing woman being no less innocent than man. Certainly, the scene between the woman and child that frames the performance would suggest that woman, like man, has fallen from grace. Equally, men and women have learnt nothing from history and repeat the same mistakes and the same acts of violence and cruelty every day. Another reading of the final scene picks up on an intertextual reference. The reference draws on another production by Odin Teatret titled *Kaosmos*: here, Torgeir Wethal (the actor playing Faust) plays a man who has spent his life waiting to be allowed past a door. At the end of *Kaosmos* he is dressed in the same female clothing as we see in *Ego Faust*. Humiliated by the end of the play, he is forced to take on the role of 'The Bride of the

Village' as a grotesque parody of a marriage event earlier in the performance (see Figure 3.3). European Medieval plays often included a subversion of the marriage to Christ, and the inclusion of this scene in both *Kaosmos* and *Ego Faust* could be read as a marriage to the devil. Arguably, in *Ego Faust*, this is an apt punishment for a man who had treated women so carelessly.

The figure of the peasant woman causes a different kind of rupture in the performance. Whereas the other performers are using an acculturated, codified performance style, she performs everyday, menial actions. She returns to the stage towards the end of the performance, once the other characters have left and Faust is taken through the door to Hell. Julia Varley has emerged from the Mr Peanut costume and gently holds the skeletal figure, dressed like Faust, in her arms. The peasant woman takes the skeletal figure in her arms and weeps.

**Figure 3.3** Finale of *Ego Faust* with Augusto Omolú and Roberta Carreri as Mephistopheles, Julia Varley as Mr Peanut and Torgeir Wethal dressed in female attire as Faust. Photograph by Fiora Bemporad

**Figure 3.4**  *Kaosmos*, 1993. Torgeir Wethal (dressed as in Figure 3.3),
Julia Varley (as Doña Musica), Jan Ferslev and Iben Nagel
Rasmussen. Photograph by Jan Rüsz

The peasant woman's everyday mode of performance bridges the gap
between the fictional world depicted on the stage and the everyday. As
she grieves for her lost love, the young girl again comes running onto
the stage, from the audience, towards the woman. The woman once
again rejects the child and beats her. The actions of the woman are
horrific, performed in silence, without emotional response. The woman
and girl are, again, dressed in everyday western clothes. The scene
presents the audience with a dilemma, as it does not fit with the rest
of the performance. It is a thematic rupture, but as a frame to the Faust
story, it invites us to read the event as a potential metaphor of power,
exploitation, human tragedy and vulnerability. Faust is a myth and this
act has the quality of the everyday. As an action it could be read as a
bridge between the world of the myth and the world of the everyday.
Barba has said that this coda is still in a very raw form but he wanted
the audience to enter and exit the experience of the performance via
the same scene, which for him demonstrates an act of absolute evil.

## LEVEL 4: IDEOLOGICAL READABILITY (SHIFTERS)

The final vector of the model, (4), is referred to as the level of 'ideological readability', or consensus. It is at this point that emphasis is put on the spectator's creative and interactive role having proceeded through levels 1, 2 and 3 and gathered information. Pavis acknowledges that the consensus or reading is based on the individual's experience, mediated through a core of cultural knowledge inherent in the performance. Therefore, even if the spectator does not have a specific understanding of the cultural tradition being performed, knowledge will have been gained through the experience of the performance, and this will have permeated through to the spectator's perception. In our adaptation of Pavis's model, we have already taken the analysis further by undertaking research into some of the different cultural practices and textual references, to develop our understanding of the performance. In his analysis, Pavis focuses on the ISTA performance of *The Island of Labyrinths*, a previous ISTA version of *Ego Faust*, and concludes that the performance is not a hybrid but a federative example of intercultural work. The notion of 'federative' demonstrates how the different cultural practices from Brazil, Bali, India and Japan are not merged into something different. They remain intact and are viewed equally, rather than in a hierarchical order, whereby one might be suggested as being better than another. The different performance styles are, however, all part of an encompassing frame, like the federation of nation states in Europe, and are governed by the same network or framework of rules. The same idea of 'federative' can be used to describe *Ego Faust*. The framework here is the coherent narrative that follows the Faust myth and this holds the different performance practices together.

As well as encouraging us to develop our thoughts on some of the aspects of the performance, this final section also invites us to pose further questions. We might now read the performance space as a metaphor for the world, with the fragments of the cultural practices creating a world of disorder and diversity, although we might also argue that this reading appears essentially reductive and overly simplistic. As Pavis has said of the work by the Theatrum Mundi Ensemble, it only brings the performers together spatially, in actuality it reflects a sense of disquiet for the spectator, in terms of how we can and should view any cultural product. Not only are the performers and performances dislocated from their culture, but so, too, are the spectators.

As spectators we are transported into a fictional space that is not wholly familiar to us.

As an example of intercultural performance, *Ego Faust* can be argued as highly successful because the disjunctive relationships created between the performers and musicians from different cultural practices create gaps or ruptures. These ruptures disorientate, or alienate, the spectator and so we become active makers of meaning, rather than passive receivers. A counter argument might say that for the spectator, who has little familiarity with different cultural practices, the performance will remain a colourful spectacle, where the unfamiliar antics are typical of strange, foreign people. Rather than being empowered by the unfamiliar, the spectator becomes disaffected. Intercultural performance can create new cultural territory where the cultural diversity in the world is celebrated, but this territory must be accessible to the spectator. In an interview, Patrice Pavis commented that there is a level of naivety about the work (1995). He suggested that some critics might argue that the performance is irresponsible in its refusal to be didactic, and that its lack of commitment to a moral or political ideology is unacceptable at this point in history but, as has already been discussed, Barba believes that theatre should resist the temptation to be swayed by the 'spirit of the times'. Theatre does not necessarily resolve problems and issues but should raise an awareness that they exist. Certainly, *Ego Faust*, as an ISTA performance, has moved on from when Pavis was asked about the work and clearly raises many issues regarding greed, the power of corruption, exploitation of women and the idea that things are rarely what they seem. We are invited to make connections between old stories and our lives now. The performance invites us to make connections with different associated narratives. For example, the playing of Margherita by a Japanese performer might remind some of us of the story of **Madame Butterfly**; subsequently, this association leads us to consider issues regarding the colonial aspects of history.

One of the initial questions considered concerned itself with the interplay of cultural references and intercultural performance. Each session of ISTA has initiated changes to the Theatrum Mundi performance score and the Italian academic, Ferdinando Taviani, notes that in 1987, 'Barba fused these scenes into a unitary framework, giving them the rhythm and energy of a homogeneous performance, something carnivalesque, funny and ritualistic' (in Hastrup, 1996: 72). In a conversation with Taviani, he pointed out that there are certain features of the performance that now have a regular place. These features include the singing of a song, which has now become an anthem for ISTA, titled 'Subo al Triquete'. The words come from a Walt Whitman poem sung in Spanish, to a melody composed by an ISTA participant; here, the composer sought to compose a work that suited both western and eastern voices. Another feature that has been incorporated into the fabric of the ISTA performance is the inclusion of a Bob Dylan song. Both the Whitman and Dylan songs accompany the moment where Margherita becomes maddened by her actions and as a consequence 'dies'. In some versions of the Theatrum Mundi performance the participants at ISTA sing the 'Subo al Triquete' anthem from the auditorium. At this point the confusion on the stage spills out into the audience. Both songs are beautiful, lyrical songs but in the context of the chaos and confusion of the scene, they become haunting and melancholic. For the spectator who is confused by the cultural references, this moment does not alleviate that confusion but does offer them an opportunity to be a participant in the carnivalesque world of the performance.

The 'consensus' at level 4 is not a resolution of all the questions that have been posed but a bringing together of what we know from the different levels of readability, to construct a level of what Pavis refers to as 'cultural readability'. The montage of scenes woven together by Barba to create the performance is as intertextual as it is intercultural. At this final level of the model we can reflect on how we have created a specific framework of analysis for this performance.

## FINAL THOUGHTS

Barba identifies three different dramaturgies in the construction of a performance, which all occur simultaneously, and do not only involve the text or the story. Observe how the three compositional strategies used by Barba in a performance equate to the four levels of Pavis's model for analysis. Barba's dramaturgies are:

1. An *organic or dynamic dramaturgy* which is in the composition of the rhythms and dynamisms affecting the spectators on a nervous, sensorial and sensual level;

2. A *narrative dramaturg*, which interweaves events and characters, informing the spectators on the meaning of what they are watching;

3. [A] *dramaturgy of changing states*, when the entirety of what we show manages to evoke something totally different.

(Barba, 2000b: 60)

The performance progresses in a linear fashion but there are numerous ruptures woven into the texture of the performance from the different threads of logic provided by the performers. Each performer demonstrates a different 'dynamic dramaturgy' that can be identified by isolating and observing the way in which a specific performer uses energy to create their scenic presence. A 'narrative dramaturgy' is clearly located as the performers in *Ego Faust* play figures that are not derived from the same fictional world. For example, we have the character of Faust but also Mr Peanut, Barong and Kleist's bear. Through the process of interweaving the performers' individual narratives, Barba constructs a frame, or world, that holds all the threads or stories and characters together. In this fictional world there are moments where the characters come together, their narratives may collide or there may be fleeting physical or musical encounters that resonate outwards to affect other characters or actions and, most of all, affect the sensibilities of the spectator.

A 'dramaturgy of changing states' is more difficult to define but equates to Pavis's level of 'ideological readability'. During the performance the spectators are held in a transitory state, a space that Victor Turner refers to as a **liminal** space (see Turner, 1986, and Schechner, 1985). A liminal space is a place between one place and another. The spectators are actually seated outside a public building in Germany but have been theatrically transported from that everyday world to another fictional world, peopled with many strange but engaging characters. Their perception of the space around them and the world they live in has been disrupted. Theatre engages us in a vibrant colourful world where we are offered the opportunity to 'experience the experience' (Barba, 1990: 100), that is, go beyond our experience of the everyday and be challenged by a heightened sense of experience.

Barba tightly choreographs the performance from the material sequences proposed by each of the actors. The spectator's ability to read, or follow, the performance is challenged because the characters and/or narratives are dislocated, or defamiliarised, from their usual context by, for example, disrupting the relationship between performers and musicians.

As a director, Barba considers himself to be the first spectator and it is the spectator who is at the core of his theatre. Spectators are an integral part of the creative celebration and we also have a dramaturgical role to perform, as Barba has outlined in his article 'Four Spectators' (1990). Here, he says that it is necessary to assume how at least three spectators will react, and to imagine a fourth (the three reactions are listed in Chapter 1).

My first reaction as a spectator was what Barba describes as 'the spectator who thinks s/he doesn't understand but who, in spite of him/herself, dances' (Barba, 1990: 99).

Performance is set apart from our everyday lives; it is something that is to be shared by those participating and those witnessing the event. Although there may be no definitive meaning for the performance that will be taken away by each and every spectator, the shared experience of having been present is potentially collective, what Victor Turner would describe as 'communitas' (see Turner, 1974: 202).

The understanding, derived from the Odin actor's training over 30 years, and the research from ISTA, constitutes a particular notion of how theatre does and can work, and this has been made concrete in their theatre practice. Barba says that for theatre to be creative it will weave a 'labyrinthine path between chaos and cosmos, with sudden swerves, paralysing stops, and unexpected solutions' (Barba, 2000b: 60). What we are presented with is a style that both references established performance practices but also disrupts these references, as, in their reconstituted and distorted forms, they become new: something that is simultaneously familiar and unfamiliar. As spectators we can delight in what we experience, recognising a multitude of moments while the whole may remain elusive. For Barba, the intention is to create a harmony between the experience and the theatre that will lead to 'an impulse to change oneself' (1986a: 15). Barba admits that the actor's process of transformation is difficult to explain, as the essence is buried beneath methodology; that the very necessity of trying to teach, to transmit knowledge, is reductive and is unable to communicate the essential. Yet, this process has become as important as the work itself: 'it is one's duty to speak precisely because the essential is mute' (1986a: 17).

*Ego Faust* can be described as spectacle as it employs music, dance and elaborate and colourful costumes. At this superficial level of spectacle, the performance is entertaining as it includes moments of humour and pathos. Although we may not be sure of what precisely is going on, we can still respond on an emotional level to the music and movement of the performance. However, the spectacle, or entertainment, level is a surface level of receiving a performance and, as developing scholars of theatre, we need to be exploring the network of communications that take us beyond the surface level of the work. The network of communications employed by the performance forms the networks of meanings that we interpret according to our own experiences. These can be broken down into further sub-divisions, for example individual readings and cultural codes: shared understandings that we have as a result of being a part of a particular cultural group. As we have seen in our analysis of the *Ego Faust* performance, the dramaturgies are very complex and invite spectators to delve more deeply. If you are a spectator who did not think you understood the performance, enjoy the freedom that the performance offers you 'to dance'.

# 4

# PRACTICAL
# EXERCISES

Barba first became involved with theatre in 1960. Over the 40 years that he has written, discussed and made theatre, and been involved with theatricality, his ideas have evolved and inevitably been changed and amended. Through the course of the book we have traced the ways in which his ideas and practices have developed, explored the common characteristics in his work and the ideas and questions he has been concerned with, from the very beginning through to the present. Key ideas and practices have been accumulated that will help you to develop your own theatre practice. The first key ideas encountered in Chapter 1 were the words 'energy' and 'action'. These words have recurred throughout this book and in order to appreciate Barba's work and approach to theatre there is a need to explore what the terms mean in practice. These two words will at various times be familiar, while at other times they can appear difficult to understand, even dull, but hopefully inspiring as well. Western theatre practice has, for a long time, been involved with ideas of progress, that is the need to constantly be changing and moving forwards. One of the implications resulting from our fascination with progress, and all things new, is that we are unused to remaining focused on one thing for very long. The long-term repetition of exercises and detailed precision of performance work can be especially challenging but it is central to Barba's work. There will be times when theatre work appears easy and you want to move on quickly to something new; there will be other times when you cannot muster the energy to repeat the exercises again; times when you realise that you actually have not connected with the work at all; and times when familiar exercises suddenly seem too difficult. However, there will be other times when you hit a moment of revelation through the exercises, times when you connect and learn something new about yourselves as performers and theatre-makers.

The idea of self-reflection is also important to our understanding of Barba's work. It is a skill that you need to develop, not just when you are training to be a performer or rehearsing for a performance, but also when you are reading and thinking about theatre. Much of the work that Barba has developed with his actors demands that they are able to reflect and think about what they are doing. Reflection enables them to identify how they have arrived at where they are and where the further challenges will be in their work. Training is a very complex process that can be helped by having someone else watching you, helping you to be reflective and checking that you are working effectively with the exercises. When working with the following exercises always try to work with someone else.

This chapter is divided into four sections:

1   *Training*: the first section will look at introductory work and ideas for training exercises that explore particular aspects of Barba's and Odin's practice. Except where stated, all of the exercises come from workshops given by Roberta Carreri.
2   *Developing material*: the second section will look at structures of workshops given by members of the Odin Teatret. These workshops explore aspects of training and approaches to creating material that could be developed as performance scores.
3   *Layering textual material*: the third section will look at developing a personal performance score and subscore.
4   *Applying the Odin approach to a text*: the final section is an account of two work demonstrations given by members of Odin, where the actors demonstrate how their approach to acting might be applied to working with given texts.

As practitioners of theatre we must be clear about what techniques we have and need before we can begin to apply our craft in one of the many different niches of, what Barba calls, the 'theatre eco-system':

> It is not the method that is important but the teacher who teaches – and then it is not the teacher but the pupil who is most important and how the pupil absorbs and transforms information, how the pupil embodies and transforms knowledge.
>
> (Barba in Odin Week, 2001)

What Barba is saying here is that you must find a way of knowing your everyday self in order to change or transform your everyday self. You can do this partly by noting how each exercise you do contains information that allows you to change. Before you begin to explore the exercises in practice, there are a few pieces of advice that Barba has given that are particularly important at this initial stage. The first piece of advice is on tiredness.

Barba tells us that we should work with tiredness as a companion; rather than striving to avoid tiredness he says that we should embrace it. By continually working for the same length of time both your physical and mental ability to work for longer periods becomes dulled, as a result if you are accustomed to classes of 45 minutes then that will be the length of your concentration. You should try as much as is possible to work for differing lengths of time and push through tiredness because sometimes you feel tired merely because you have stopped concentrating. Tiredness can also come through the repetition of an exercise. You need to find ways of challenging and stimulating yourself so that you remain alert when working. It is too easy to repeat an exercise for a few minutes, decide that you have achieved what is necessary from the exercise and become dull to the work. It is not the exercise that is necessarily at fault but your attitude to the exercise. If you become quickly bored with the work you might make changes to the rhythm or the dynamic of the exercise, so presenting yourself with new challenges. To work through the lethargy can often lead to remarkable results and discoveries about your ability; however, there is a point where you merely repeat an exercise mechanically. When you have taken an exercise as far as you can you need to move on to find a new challenge. The training work is something that you should do every day. It is repetitious and demands discipline and should always be challenging.

With all the exercises on the following pages you need to ensure that you work safely. Ensure that you wear loose fitting clothes, no jewellery, that the space, as far as possible, is clear of obstacles, clean and that, as far as is practical, you always work in bare feet. Some of the exercises are to be done alone and some require you to work with someone else. Whatever combination you are working in, you need to have a responsibility to the whole group working in the space at all times. If you are struggling to remain focused on the work then ensure you do not disrupt the work that others are trying to do. Accidents can happen when people lose concentration. Always ensure you work with *soft knees*, again you can injure yourself by having unnecessary tensions in your body. Soft knees means not locking your knees but having them slightly bent. Initially, this position may feel awkward and this is the first step towards changing yourself from your everyday self. Although it may appear easy to stand:

- legs apart, feet about the distance of a fist apart;
- knees slightly bent – or soft;
- ankles soft;
- shoulders relaxed;
- spine upright but soft, strong and actively balanced;
- breathing evenly;

you will find that maintaining this relaxed but active and alert position, while doing the work, may become difficult. Ensure that every so often you check yourself. An essential part of the work is learning to be self-reflective. As Barba says at the beginning, what is important is how you, the pupil, embody and transform yourself using the exercises. We must first learn to know ourselves.

## SECTION 1: TRAINING

The following is a checklist of things that you need to remember both when you are working on training in the workspace and when you are performing theatre. Standing in the space check that:

- the knees are soft;
- shoulders relaxed;
- chest open;
- toes are not tense;
- legs are apart;
- spine is upright but soft.

Check that you feel well balanced. Reflect on your breathing. Reflect on what parts of the body move as you breathe in and out. Now reflect on your spine.

We will begin by exploring movement from the spine. By making small, soft movements note the base of your spine and then follow the spine upwards, slowly feeling the effect of small movements to the spine, all the way up to the point where the spine meets the head. Continue to experiment with the ways in which a slight movement from the spine can lead, like a set of ripples on water, to larger movements in other parts of the body.

## Exercise 4.1: 'The snake dance'

This exercise comes from part of a workshop given by Roberta Carreri. She uses a piece of music called 'The Upside Down Guitar' by composer Michael Nyman and asks the participants to imagine that their spine is a snake, a cobra. Using this image of the cobra, the participants are asked to respond to the music by letting the snake inside slowly begin to awaken and dance.

### What to do

➤ Standing on a spot, the *snake dance* begins in the spine, and the eyes. (Roberta refers to the eyes as 'the last vertebra'.)

➤ The eyes begin with a soft focus but are ready to change focus, reacting to the impulses in the music. Begin to look around the space.

➤ The spine (including the eyes) slowly begins to move and the movement becomes more intense as it responds to the music.

➤ Remaining on the spot, allow the movements to become slowly bigger and bigger until finally you need to let the snake move in the space.

➤ Then slowly reduce and reduce the movement until you are once again moving on the spot, taking the dance back inside of you.

➤ Remember to constantly be working with the eyes as a part of your spine. You are letting your 'snake' dance.

➤ Remember a snake has no arms or legs; this does not mean that you hold your arms rigidly by your sides but that your body should follow the momentum initiated from the spine.

➤ Remember it is the momentum of both the music and the movement that forces you to let the snake go and dance around the whole space.

### What to note

As noted, in the *snake dance* the eyes are very important and clearly indicate when you are 'in the moment', or merely going through the motions of an exercise or performance. We can appear to be looking out but actually we are reflecting inwardly on something completely different. The first part of the spine exercise requires you to be looking on the inside, whereas the *snake dance* requires you to be looking on the outside. It may be useful to practise the shift between looking on the inside (where the intensity of your focus is very soft) to looking on the outside (where the intensity of your focus becomes stronger and stronger – burning in to a point that you have fixed your gaze upon).

The *snake dance* requires that you do two things simultaneously: actively looking and responding to the music. This can often be more of a problem than we would like to let on! As with anything else it demands practice.

### Developments

Play with hard eyes and soft eyes, using the eyes to burn into a fixed point and then using the eyes seductively, so making the eyes and spine work with the largest possible movements and then reducing the movements down to the smallest perceptible movements; always ensuring that the level of intensity is clear and comes from your response to the music.

### Connections

This exercise requires you to work with different qualities of energy and connects with the terms anima, animus and **keras** and **manis** – check in the glossary if you have forgotten what the terms mean.

## Exercise 4.2: 'The hunter'

Be 'in the moment', be in the action and be prepared. You need to be alert, ready, listening and looking. Ensure that you are *really* looking around the space and listening, and *really* alert, rather than going through the motions!

### What to do

➤ Begin in a squat position.

➤ Ensure you are ready to move.

- ➤ Actively look and listen.
- ➤ Immediately you hear the clap of hands, jump, being decided in that moment on where you are turning.
- ➤ Land in the squat position, facing a different direction.
- ➤ Continue to look and listen, immediately be ready to jump again.
- ➤ Repeat.

## What to note

Ensure when you jump you land softly and quietly. You are like a hunter in a forest, listening and looking, and on the impulse 'change' being able to efficiently move. It is important to fight against the desire to pre-determine where you will move – be 'in the moment'. If you are thinking where you will land, you will not be looking and listening. In theatre we work with illusion but we need to remember that theatre takes place in actual time and space so, although the events may be a fiction, the actions need to be real, not realistic. The hunter exercise is not about pretending to look and listen it is about actually looking and listening, and being 'in the moment'.

## Developments

Pause and take stock: how many times did you forget to keep your knees soft? How often did you check that you were not tensing the neck and shoulders? How often did you check your breathing? Where were the challenges for you in the exercises and how might you work on improving your ability? Remember to carry across the work on the spine, the eyes, looking, listening to the next area of work.

How long were you able to sustain your energy and focus before becoming tired? Next time try to extend the exercise for a longer period.

## Connections

The exercise aims to explore the idea of sats. The idea of sats is demon-strated in this exercise because sats is precisely concerned with working with impulses: an action does not begin with the jump itself but in the energy and focus used in the preparation to jump. There needs to be a precise intention in the actor's movement, the body needs to be *decided* and aware of other people's decisions; most of all it is vital not to antici-pate or predetermine what you intend to do.

## Exercise 4.3: 'Precarious balance'

The three principles of the pre-expressive are, you will remember, alter-ation in balance, the law of opposition and coherent incoherence.

As Barba says, 'the performer's life is based on an alteration of balance' (1995: 18). In many cultures, performers change their everyday balance to create what Barba has called an extra-daily or 'luxury' balance and this new balance might be considered to be unstable and in opposition to our 'natural' balance. In chapter three of *The Paper Canoe*, Barba outlines how some codified performance practices use different techniques to walk by using different parts of their feet.

Before we begin exploring different ways of standing and walking we should remind ourselves that we have feet!

### *What to do*
➤   Stand straight and look in front of you.
➤   With the left foot flat on the floor, place the tip of the right big toe to the floor.
➤   Push down slowly through the toe to the ball of the foot.
➤   As the ball of the right foot has contact with the floor, slowly lift the left foot from the floor, keeping the toes pointed towards the floor.
➤   Continue to push the weight and energy down through the right foot to the heel and now place the tip of the left big toe on the floor.
➤   Exchange weight from the left over to the right.
➤   Repeat transferring weight and balance back and forth from the left foot back to the right and so forth.

### *What to note*
Remember to work very slowly but fluidly; check the precision of each movement in the exercise. Ensure that the balance is maintained and that the whole body is engaged in the exercise. Initially, work on the exer-cise as though you are in slow motion, so that any problems the body has can be identified and solved. To ensure that you keep the pace of the exercise slow you might do the exercise to the count of eight. Speed up as you find a rhythm but do not lose the precision of each part of the movement.

### *Developments*
Now that you have warmed your feet up, try moving around the space using different parts of your foot in contact with the floor, for example:

- ➤ the inside of the foot;
- ➤ the outside of the foot;
- ➤ the heel;
- ➤ the ball of the foot;
- ➤ toes raised;
- ➤ toes scrunched up;
- ➤ try different rhythms, for example, gliding, spiky, heavy, precise, hesitant movement;
- ➤ try keeping your knees together as you walk, keep the steps small and remember to keep the spine upright but soft and active.

### Connections

Each time you explore a different way of walking or moving around the space, begin slowly and reflect on how the different balance affects your whole body. It is very important with all the work you do that you are aware of how the whole body is engaged and affected by even the smallest adjustments or changes. Reflect on how the changes affect the way you look around the space, breathe, use your arms and hands. You might refer to *The Paper Canoe* (p. 18) to see how Barba documents different traditions and how they stand or walk.

## Exercise 4.4: 'Jumping'

Another seemingly simple exercise, that again requires us to reflect on a familiar action and how we use energy, is jumping.

### What to do

- ➤ Standing on the spot, jump up.
- ➤ Standing on the spot, jump down.
- ➤ Remember to keep your knees and ankles soft.
- ➤ Repeat.

### What to note

There is a difference between jumping up rather than jumping down – this is not about height but energy. If we jump down we land heavily, whereas if we jump up we land lightly and quietly. Try the difference between jumping when you send the energy upwards and when you jump down, letting the energy fall.

### Connection

If we consider here the second principle of the pre-expressive, the law of opposition, we can identify how jumping illustrates the way in which the law operates. In order for the body to leave the ground and spring upwards the first movement we need to make is downwards. We bend our knees and direct energy down in order to then push it up and jump. The more that we can be aware of how we use energy the more in control of energy we can be and the more efficient we can then be.

### Additional note

Return to 'The hunter' exercise, where you were required to squat and jump. Try the exercise again, reflecting on how you control and focus the energy.

## Exercise 4.5: 'The result of necessity'

The next exercise explores ways of moving by leading with a part of the body and is an exercise that many of you may be familiar with. This is a very difficult exercise as, again, the temptation is to imitate or play at doing, rather than actually doing. The aim of the exercise is to break away from mannered behaviour and to achieve a working together of the mind and body.

### What to do

➤ Start by standing straight, with your knees slightly bent (you should have the feeling that there is a line going from the top of your head, through your body to a point between your heels).

➤ Respond to an imaginary line pulling you forward from your fore-head, taking you away from your centre of gravity (see Figure 4.1).

➤ Take a step.

➤ Now reflect on where the action of stepping began and at what point in the action your balance changed and necessitated you taking the step.

➤ Standing upright but balanced, focus on a part of the body that you are going to use to create the necessity of moving.

➤ Slowly continue to work from your head before you move on to try, for example, an elbow, nose, left hip, and move it until you feel the impulse to step.

➤ Move the body off balance – see what happens, how far can the body follow an impulse before the impulse to take a step occurs?

**Figure 4.1** Roberta Carreri demonstrating during a workshop in the 'closed' session at ISTA, 2000. Photograph by Fiora Bemporad

➤ Before taking the next step, find the necessity or impulse to move by taking the body off its new balance.

➤ Try taking three or four steps before changing direction.

➤ Move both forwards and backwards and around.

➤ Keep movements continuous and fluid – always decided and always in the moment.

➤ Alternate big impulses with small impulses, big steps with small steps.

### What to note

Each time you begin leading with a different part of the body, begin slowly and fully explore the adjustments your body needs to make. The body should always be working from a point of active balance that entails the spine being soft and active, not rigid or passive. The impulse to change direction should come from a new part of your body taking over the lead.

Do not blur the distinctions between one impulse and another. Take time in the exercise; the tendency can be to speed up and the movements become less decided and less distinct and precise. Ensure that when you move you take steps, rather than fall from one place to another. Find fluidity in the movement and try not to re-establish your position after each movement (try not to bring your feet together after a step but let the foot that has taken the step be in front), for example, halting the movement and losing the energy, and then having to begin again to find the impulse to move.

This exercise is not about sticking out an elbow or shoulder and moving around the space, but finding the necessity or impulse to move – what Roberta calls, leading the body out of its 'baricenter'. Be careful not to compensate, or pull back, when you move off balance, otherwise you will lose the necessity to move. Moving while merely sticking out an elbow or chin is a sign that you are not taking the body off balance, off its centre, so ensure that the leading and necessity to move are real.

A tendency, when doing this exercise, is either to focus so intensely on the doing that we stop seeing in the space or, as the movement becomes more fluid, we get carried away and we stop thinking and deciding where the movement should go. It is too easy for us to think we can work in autopilot and stop thinking. It is easy to bluff. If we do, we quickly return to old habits and old patterns of behaviour; we are learning nothing.

### Developments

➤ Change the parts of your body you choose to lead the impulse: use round lines and curves, not just straight lines.

➤ Keep changing the rhythm of the work, avoid anticipating and maintain the precision of the actions.

➤ Check whether you are falling and then re-establishing, or whether you are genuinely finding the necessity of the movement.

➤ Leading with the heart entails very small movements and should not be confused with moving the shoulders or hips.

➤ Alternate between leading movement from the head, the shoulders and the heart.

This exercise, although a training exercise, can be adapted and applied to performance work.

➤ In pairs stand at opposite sides of a room and each adopt characters from a play you both know, for example, Jean and Miss Julie from Strindberg's play *Miss Julie*, Agamemnon and Clytemnestra from Aeschylus' play of *The Oresteia*, or Gertrude and Hamlet from Shakespeare's play *Hamlet*.

➤ Each of you should select three different parts of the body that will lead your impulse to move.

➤ Slowly walk towards each other, meet and then move away from each other.

➤ You might repeat this exercise several times to explore using the impulses in the walk differently.

➤ Observe what your partner is doing and respond, that means build a physical dialogue with each other.

➤ Finally, reflect on what information has been revealed about the characters and their relationship.

### Connections

Being in the moment, being decided, pre-expressive notions of opposition and alteration of balance.

## Exercise 4.6: 'Dynamic mobility'

### What you need to do

➤ Start by standing straight, with your knees slightly bent, and feel the line, or axis, going through your body from the top of your head to a point between your heels.

➤ Gently stretch out your spine from the top of your head through to the tip of your tail.

➤ Start to move in the space by letting the whole spine move forward, caressing the floor with your feet.

➤ Let your feet glide in front, behind and around as you explore moving in straight lines and curved lines; always gliding through the space.

➤ You should frequently change direction and as you do this your movements will become almost like a waltz, whirling around the space.

➤ Keep the knees bent and the spine soft.

➤ Remember to do, to think and to be aware of the space and the presence of others around you.

➤ At the command 'stop', the body should stop but the dynamic of the movement should continue inside, this means that you continue to think and do the action although immobile.

➤ Hold this internal movement for as long as you can before moving off again.

➤ Continue to move, stop, hold and go.

➤ See how long you can hold before another thought enters your head and you are distracted.

### What to note

Keep the movements as flowing as possible. Keep your centre of gravity as low as possible and enjoy the sensation of gliding around the space.

### Connections

As previously noted in Chapter 2, this exercise illustrates an internal/external example of the pre-expressive concept of opposition, the idea, from Beijing Opera, of 'movement stop, inside no stop' (Barba, 1995: 58), used in connection with sats, and the way in which we might understand the sub-divisions of *jo-ha-kyu*.

## Exercise 4.7: 'Active balance and soft resistance'

The next series of exercises requires you to explore movement in slow motion.

### What you need to do

➤ Imagine that you are moving under water.

➤ Take giant steps to avoid stepping on the beautiful coral gardens.

➤ Use the resistance of the water to inform all of your movements.

➤ Direct your energy, move in a decided way, be precise and keep balance and fluidity of movement.

➤ As you begin, take an enormous step but only touch the floor with the tip of your toe before you transfer the weight of your body onto that foot.

➤ Remember to always keep the spine, knees and ankles soft when you are working.

➤ You should never be stationary when doing this exercise.

### What to note

Feel the resistance of the very heavy water and use your body to push against the water; check that your hands are also feeling the resistance. Keep a balance between visualising the fictional landscape and really looking. Think about the oppositions in the body, if your leg is going one way, the arms should be going in an opposite direction; the torso might be going backwards and an arm might be moving forwards. You need to do this in order to keep the balance. There should be no tension in the face. Remember, in order to stand up, the law of opposition indicates that you will first need to find a counterbalance, or counter-direction, in which to move. The shortest path between two points is not always possible, nor an interesting path to take. Explore moving using more circuitous routes. With each sequence keep the movement precise, very slow and controlled. Find ways of solving problems of moving. Observe the transitions of weight needed to move from sitting to standing. Ensure you keep your focus outside.

### Developments

➤ In the world of slow motion find three different ways of sitting and three different ways of standing, without touching the floor with your hands.

➤ Create a movement sequence incorporating the different ways of standing and sitting.

➤ As you repeat the process of standing and sitting in the sequence, do not stop thinking just because the sequence has become familiar.

➤ The weight should never be on the two feet at the same time, as the two feet should never be on the floor at the same time, unless you are doing the action of standing up or sitting down.

➤ In order to move from sitting to standing, explore ways of moving forward, sideways or back.

➤ Concentrate on displacing your weight, rather than moving in straight lines.

### Additional advice

Roberta advises that when we intend to stand up we should think 'down', and when we intend to sit down we should think 'up'. She says that this creates a resistance that will enable you to move with your whole body. Try this and see how it affects your movement and how you focus energy.

### Connections

This exercise employs all three of the principles of the pre-expressive.

## Exercise 4.8: 'Thought body'

In Roberta's second season of training at Odin, she was able to create her own principles of training. For inspiration she watched the work of other theatre groups, read books, looked at photographs, significantly of old men playing the French game of petanque (see Carreri, 2000: 56). In her training Roberta tried to create a physical equivalent to the pictures of the men throwing the small balls. She did this by creating 'snapshots' of actions using the principle of equivalence (see Figure 4.2; here, Roberta is working with the action of throwing).

Roberta would explore many different ways of throwing for maybe 30 minutes at a time. With each action, as the energy of the action moved forward, she would hold onto it in a frozen moment before releasing it. When working with any particular principle of training there are five elements that can be worked with to vary the exercise, combat tiredness, and create new challenges and these are *rhythm*, *intensity*, *pace*, *direction* and *size*.

### What you need to do

➤ Working with a partner, actually throw and catch a tennis ball between you and freeze the moment each time the ball is released and caught.

➤ Working alone, improvise throwing a ball.

➤ Movement should be continuous throughout the whole exercise.

➤ Continue with the improvising and work with changing the dynamics of rhythm, intensity, pace, direction and size.

➤ Repeat the above, improvising catching a ball.

### What to note

This exercise, and the following development exercise, is aimed at developing your body knowledge. The exercises build your ability to mould your use of presence in different ways and to think with your whole body. You are developing your ability to work with precision, opposition and resistance. All of these elements are essential for us to be able to effectively engage energy and, thus, the attention of the

**Figure 4.2** Roberta Carreri working, here demonstrating the idea of a 'snapshot', 1993. Photograph by Tony D'Urso

spectator. The exercises are described as movement dialogues of listening and telling without words. Again, note where you are not thinking together, where one of you is merely demonstrating the action and their whole body is not engaged. 'Real' actions usually use more energy and have more presence than demonstration. When an actor is merely demonstrating, and is not focused with her/his whole body, the energy does not flow and the work is not compelling or interesting to watch.

### Development
➤   In pairs, face each other, hands together and begin to push.
➤   Explore different ways of pushing: strongly or softly, up or down – listen to the impulses from your partner and be ready to respond.
➤   Start to move around the space.
➤   Do not lean on each other but explore the giving and taking of resistance.
➤   Repeat the exercise but this time lace your fingers together and pull rather than push.
➤   Develop the exercise to move between pulling and pushing.
➤   As you continue to repeat the exercise, moving in the space, develop and begin to fix moments in the flow that you both consider interesting.
➤   Find four still moments.
➤   You will need to rewind to find out how you got into the position – this is especially important as it develops the physical memory.
➤   Do not use words to find and fix.
➤   Create a sequence incorporating the four still moments.

### Connections
All of the above exercises begin to help you explore real action, and begin to give you an embodied understanding of physical memory, for example, through the resistance created by the body of your partner. The exercises show you how you can learn to focus and sustain physical and mental presence and, as you have read, Barba believes scenic presence to be a key to attracting and keeping the attention of the spectator.

# SECTION 2: DEVELOPING MATERIAL

The following are all based on complete workshops given by members of Odin during Odin Weeks between 2001 and 2002.

## Workshop 4.1: 'Making a small poem with your body'
(derived from Iben Nagel Rasmussen. One and a half hours)

As we have already realised from the previous section, all exercises evoke a particular energy and Iben's workshop is concerned with working slowly, with a soft resistance. This workshop usefully follows on from the previous work, introduced by Roberta. The energy you are going to use in the workshop is earthbound, strong, and the balance is again precarious, that is, working against our daily balance.

### *What you need to do*
➤ In pairs with a strip of cloth about a metre and a half long between each pair, select who will be Person A and Person B.
➤ Person A places the cloth across the hips of Person B and firmly holds each end while standing behind them.
➤ Both A and B should adopt a physical posture similar to sitting on an upright chair with the important difference that the energy A is using is moving forward, whereas B's energy is holding back.
➤ Person A should feel the point of resistance against the cloth and begin to move forward keeping that resistance at all times.
➤ Person B responds to the resistance and follows where Person A leads.
➤ Both should keep their knees bent, back upright and the movement slow.
➤ Neither A nor B should be pulling but working with resistance.
➤ Continue to explore moving with the cloth across the hips for 5–10 minutes, keeping steps small, movement flowing, knees together and soft, arms and neck relaxed and spine active.
➤ Now move the cloth across the chest of Person A and repeat, feeling the different resistance and noting how the change affects each part of the body.
➤ Repeat again, this time with the cloth across the forehead.

➤ Change over, with Person B leading and repeat each of the exercises. Remember to physically and mentally fix how the different experiences feel.

➤ Working individually in the space, recreate each of the positions of resistance in the body that you worked with: hips, chest and forehead, both from the position of the leader and the cloth holder. Be as precise as possible in keeping the same tension and energy in your movements, note how this experience is different without the cloth.

### What to note

As well as working with resistance this exercise is also about working with body memory. It is important that, as well as doing the exercise and working in the moment, both A and B note how the resistance and movement affect their body.

Always check your physical posture and keep the sitting position, remember to breathe and to look outwards, rather than look as though you are looking! Think what you need to do to recreate the movement without the cloth. What are you concentrating on? How is this different from when you were working with the cloth? When you are working on the linking movements in the development section below, ensure that you continue to use the slow walk with resistance. Keep all the movements slow and precise. Avoid creating unnecessary tension in the movement but ensure that you are always working with resistance.

### Development

➤ Return to your partner and explore as many different and interesting ways of pulling the cloth between you as you can find.

➤ Select three ways that you consider to be the most interesting or challenging.

➤ Learn and fix them, find a way of linking the three pulls.

➤ Repeat the movements with the same energy and resistance but without the cloth. Take time to do this and ensure that you keep the precision and solve the problems of moving from one pulling movement to another.

➤ With your partner explore as many different ways of using your energy to push against each other.

- ➤ Select three ways of pushing against each other that you consider to be the most interesting; again, learn and fix each push.
- ➤ Find a way of linking the three pushes together.
- ➤ Recreate the whole sequence 5 cm apart from your partner. Continue to repeat the sequence exploring how sections work both apart and then together.
- ➤ Put the pulls and pushes together into a sequence.
- ➤ Find the transitions between each of the sections.
- ➤ Try the whole score individually in the space.
- ➤ Return to your partner and explore different ways of embracing, choose two and add them into the score.
- ➤ Learn and fix.
- ➤ Do the whole score individually in the space and then return and repeat the score with your partner but 5 cm apart.
- ➤ Do the whole score but reduce the size of the actions by 50 per cent, then return to repeat the sequence at 100 per cent.
- ➤ Continue to play with the sequence, interweaving one way of working and then another. Although the size of the actions might change, the amount of effort and energy should not be diminished.

### Additional development

To develop the score further now you might individually add in a poem, a song or a piece of theatrical text.

Whisper the text as you perform the movement score. Do not worry about how the meaning of the text works with the score, but play with different rhythms and tones. Return to work with your partner and create a dialogue with the two pieces of text you are using. Again, you do not need to be concerned with whether it makes sense at this stage but enjoy experimenting with the sound and movement.

### Connection

This exercise clearly demonstrates the pre-expressive idea of equivalence. The workshop introduces you to a way of constructing a score that might be used as the basis for a performance score.

## Workshop 4.2: 'Non-verbal communication, contact and improvisation'

(Tage Larsen. One and a half hours)

Tage presents the workshop using very few words. He requires the group to carefully watch him and do what is indicated in his actions; information is rarely repeated. The work focuses on spontaneity, developing group work and creatively working with different dynamics and rhythms.

### What you need to do

➤ Group stands in a circle.
➤ Run slowly around in a circle, palms facing down, shoulders bouncing with the rhythm, feet light on the floor.
➤ The group keep this movement going throughout the rest of the exercise.
➤ A person goes into the centre of the circle and makes an improvisation.
➤ A second person goes into the centre of the circle and joins in, immediately copying what has been set up.
➤ The couple leave and another two enter and create a different improvisation using opposite energies from the previous couple.
➤ Everyone should enter the circle both as a proposer and a copier, particular information to improvise with may be given.
➤ Continue the slow running but break away from the circle.
➤ Resist a group rhythm and find contradictory rhythms in your movement.

Begin to build in encounters with others in the space:

➤ Make eye contact with someone in the space.
➤ Stop.
➤ Go down on one knee and slap your thigh. This gesture is an invitation to them to put their foot on your thigh and for you to shrug them off backwards.
➤ Once you have either shrugged or been shrugged off continue moving around the space and seek another encounter.
➤ By tapping someone on the shoulder you invite them to fall back into your waiting arms. (This is a typical trust exercise so you must be responsible in your approach to catching them.)

- ➤ Tapping an ankle. This action invites someone to link opposite ankles with you, hop three times and then join opposite hands and spin around.
- ➤ Interweaving your fingers and clasping your hands together in a gesture indicates to your partner that you are inviting them to mirror your offer of an improvisation.
- ➤ They agree by similarly clasping their hands together.
- ➤ A slap of the chest invites your chosen partner to go through your legs rock'n'roll style: holding your partner's hands, you swing them down between your legs and then pull them back through and up again.

### What to note

In the first part of the workshop, ensure that when you go into the circle, what you propose or copy is not generalised but precise and detailed. Those on the outside should maintain the slow running to a basic rhythm, keeping the feet as light as possible. (Tage describes the feet as 'flying silently'.)

You will need to be in a strong, balanced position at all times during this workshop. It is worth spending some time working in pairs to find the most effective way of making the actions work for the encounters and invitations. Begin doing the actions carefully and slowly to solve any technical problems.

Avoid absorbing your partner's weight, both when you are an inviter and when you are an invitee, always try to work efficiently. Be careful! Accidents happen when people are not aware who is behind them, when they are in someone else's way, and if they have not fixed eye contact with a partner, and gained a contract with them, before beginning the action. The workshop requires stamina and sustained concentration throughout. Losing concentration also leads to accidents. The person who makes the invitation is always the one who leads. Ensure that you remain alert at all times and that you sustain high energy levels throughout. When moving around the space, constantly look for opportunities to work with different people in different ways, and always be aware of the movement of the whole group.

### Developments

The final invitation given by Tage involved slapping your folded arms, a signal that invites your partner to place the toes of one foot carefully on your breastbone and lean in before pushing off backwards. The exercise is about collaboration rather than fighting and the actions must be performed *very* precisely. This is a typical, early exercise used by the Odin actors when training. You can see Tage working on this exercise in the video *Physical Training at Odin Teatret*.

You can continue to introduce your own developments to this exercise.

### Connections

The exercise requires you to focus your mental and physical energy. You are looking to share a common weight between you and an invited partner, and common impulses. You need to work collaboratively and need to be 'decided', always in the moment, and never blocking what someone is offering to you, otherwise accidents will happen. Working through tiredness is an important aspect to this exercise. It is often the case that when we begin an exercise, we work using too much energy and quickly become tired. We then become tired in the sense of being dulled by the repetition of the exercise. What we should be doing is developing our ability and capability of sustaining concentration and energy.

## Workshop 4.3

(derived from Julia Varley's vocal training exercises. One and a half hours)

### What you need to do

The group begins by standing in a circle. Stand in a neutral position (with your legs apart but balanced, with your shoulders, knees, spine, lips and mouth all soft but active).

As you stand, always keep a small space under your arms, as though, says Julia, you have a small bird there.

➤   Imagine air is something you can grasp and, with your hands, pluck handfuls of air from all around you and swallow it, constantly changing the rhythm and the dynamic of the movement.
➤   Work on your toes by imaginatively digging into the sand beneath your feet. Keep the sole of the foot on the floor.
➤   Lift your arms above your head as you breathe in and, as you let your arms slowly drop, breathe out.

- ➤ Repeat and make a 'shhh' sound by pushing the air out between your teeth.
- ➤ Repeat this action several times.
- ➤ In pairs, facing each other, repeat the above exercise keeping your palms together.
- ➤ Explore the pressure and resistance from pushing against your partner; do not lean against them or use your weight.
- ➤ Repeat and fix the experience; now repeat individually but with the same feeling.
- ➤ What do you notice?
- ➤ Take a breath in and, as you slowly exhale, play with the sound 'bvz', letting the sound vibrate.
- ➤ Start with a 'burr' sound and roll it over into the 'v' and then 'z' sounds.
- ➤ Continue to breathe in and exhale playing with these sounds.
- ➤ Repeat this exercise but using the sound 'mng'. Where in the mouth and head does this sound vibrate?
- ➤ Now practise rolling your b's and then your r's very fast.
- ➤ Beginning with your hand close to the floor, vocally follow your hand as it reaches as high as it can.
- ➤ Now repeat, but this time the low tones are made when the hand is high in the space and the high tones are made when the hand is low in the space.
- ➤ You might try this exercise in pairs, where one of you uses your hand to lead the other person's voice.
- ➤ Working with the opposition of high hand, low voice, follow your partner's hand.
- ➤ What do you notice about the two ways of working?

The next exercise requires you to see, or imagine you see, someone on the other side of the room; be surprised; explore the feeling of delight at seeing the imaginary person.

- ➤ Try embracing the person next to you to familiarise yourself with the feeling you are projecting towards the imaginary person.
- ➤ Repeat the exercise of seeing someone and being delighted, but use the sound 'shhh' to express the action.
- ➤ Return to the breathing exercise, raising arms and lowering them as you breathe out making the 'shhh' sound.

➤   As you continue with the exercise, imagine you have a drop of water
     on your tail.

➤   Bounce on your tail to try and lose the drop.

➤   Let the voice bounce with the movement – this time make a 'huh,
     huh, huh' sound – in this instance bounce down rather than up.

### What to note

Be aware of your body in the space. Allow the voice and the body to
work together. Make sure that you divide your energy equally between
the physical action and the vocal action. Try not to think too much
about what you are doing, as you will stop looking out and begin to put
tensions into your body and voice. Continually check yourself throughout the workshop to see whether you are tending to hold your voice,
putting tension into either your voice or body. If you are, work at letting
go of the tension, be free and released, both physically and vocally.
If you strain the voice it will become tighter and thinner. Always work
with precision. Avoid the tendency of allowing the rhythm to run out of
control, especially when an exercise requires you to frequently change
rhythms.

When working with the 'carrying' exercise below, carefully consider
where the voice was coming from when you were carrying or being
carried and work on reproducing the vocal placement. When recreating
a vocal or physical action, 'as if', a performer can over-compensate and
push the voice harder than necessary. Check that you are not forcing
the voice. Listen to others working together and then 'as if'. Listen for
the difference between the vocal tension that comes with the resistance
of working with someone and the tension that is forced, and causes a
cramp in the voice.

Building strength and trust in your voice takes time and you should
not expect too much too soon. You will often sound horrible, and you will
make mistakes, but this is part of the work. What is most important is to
stay truthful and work organically. Julia says that it can take four years
of patient work to achieve results with the voice. Progress should evolve
organically and should not be forced or achieved by distorting the voice.
You must work patiently.

When we are speaking 'naturally' there is often a greater urgency to
communicate, we are more relaxed physically and we are not thinking
technically about how we are using or placing the voice. What can we
learn from our 'natural' voice when we are speaking text? Having a

listener to monitor your behaviour can help you to identify old habits and avoid lazy behaviour, as well as preventing you from learning bad habits. Remember practice does not necessarily mean perfect. Practice can also mean permanent.

### Development

Working with a piece of spoken text. You might use the words to a nursery rhyme, a song, a poem or a speech you have learnt.

➤ Begin by walking around in the space, continue walking and begin speaking the text. Walk lightly and not heavily.

➤ Don't colour the text with any vocal intonations but allow the text to follow the rhythm of your walking.

➤ Use the voice and body together.

➤ Move and vocalise slowly. Focus on the body, not the text – remembering that the voice is a part of the body.

➤ Do not decorate the text but speak it neutrally.

➤ Continue walking and vocalising but put jumps in, remembering to jump up and not down.

➤ Continue to vocalise the text but this time skip around the room, again remembering to keep the skipping light. Don't anticipate the effect that the skipping will have on the voice but feel and respond to the changes in rhythm.

➤ Alternate between walking and skipping and ensure that the voice changes as the body changes and do not let the changes in rhythms become blurred. Be precise.

➤ Go back to walking with the text and jump, the voice should jump with the body; imagine your favourite sports team has scored the winning point!

➤ Now alternate between walking, skipping and jumping.

➤ Explore the vocal action of resistance. Vocally recreate the slow motion physical energy used with the different ways of sitting and standing from the first section.

➤ The next part of the work requires you to work in pairs of similar weight and height. Decide who will be 'A' and 'B'.

➤ 'A' is to be the weight.

➤ 'B' carries the weight.

➤ The pair should explore different ways of carrying and different ways of moving; both speaking their vocal text at the same time.

➤ 'A' should not be a dead weight but should give their weight.
➤ Explore what happens to the voice when taking the weight; do not anticipate what will happen to the voice.
➤ Repeat 'as if' carrying or being carried.
➤ Change partners.
➤ Stand facing each other, put your palms together, interlacing your fingers.
➤ Explore the movements of pulling and pushing, all the time using your spoken text.
➤ Use the voice to push and pull.
➤ Avoid leaning against your partner.
➤ Try surprising your partner.
➤ Repeat but without touching, recreating the physical and vocal action as precisely as possible.
➤ Find a different partner.
➤ Play with listening, speaking and distance.
➤ The listener should move around the space continually.
➤ The listener has permission to squeeze the speaker if they consider that their partner is straining their voice or tensing their neck.
➤ The speaker should modulate their voice in relation to where the listener is in the space.
➤ Develop the exercise by replacing the text with your own reflections on the drama work you have been doing, or any other account of your daily behaviour.
➤ Notice the differences between the 'natural' and the 'text' voice.

### Additional development

As a final exercise in the workshop each person should stand or sit on a chair.

➤ Use your text to vocally embrace the room, the whole building and then the local area outside.
➤ Use the voice to create the image of fog, snow falling in winter, a Pekinese dog making a love call to a cat in the street, water cascading down a waterfall, a Soviet leader speaking to the whole of the Red Square, a commentator at a race, a fly trying to find its way out of a room, an iceberg beginning to thaw, wind blowing across a desert.

You can add your own ideas and challenges to this exercise.

### Connections

It is important to emphasise the importance of listening to your own voice, as well as other voices, in an exercise. Learn how to identify strains, tensions and artificiality in the voice. Always listen outside of yourself. Listen to your voice coming back or, as Julia says, 'The Echo of Silence', the title of the vocal work demonstration available from Odin on video. The video contains lots of other ideas for working, and good advice.

All of the exercises created in the physical training have an equivalent in vocal training. For example, all the physical training exercises work with different types of energy, rhythm, intensity, etc., and these variations can be applied to the vocal exercises and work with vocal text. You might try finding ways of using resistance in your voice as we did in Iben's workshop. Remember, resistance is not the same as tension.

It is important to protect your voice by not pushing the voice to attain results. The voice should be reactive and not strained. Pushing and straining the voice can lead to serious damage, so ensure that you work carefully and patiently. It is important for you to find exercises that are the most appropriate for your own voice.


## SECTION 3: LAYERING TEXTUAL MATERIAL – CREATING AND WORKING WITH PERFORMANCE SCORES

### Workshop 4.4: 'The ideogram'

This workshop is derived from one given by Barba where he develops the work over several sessions. Each session lasts approximately one hour. Barba decides on a theme for the work according to the group and intention of the meeting. For example, these sessions followed the theme of 'digging beneath the surface' and were part of the ISTA work in Sweden in 1996, whereas the account in *The Paper Canoe*, that follows a similar structure, is titled 'The dark hands of oblivion' (1995: 154–172). You will need to select a theme that will suit your needs. When selecting a theme remember Barba's advice that it is important to take several steps back from where you want to be. Finding the initial theme can be difficult. The idea of 'digging beneath the surface' immediately suggests a real action, whereas 'the dark hands of oblivion' suggests something more abstract and enigmatic. Sometimes it is best to begin with a straightforward theme that has links with an action. Once the theme has been given, each individual should explore the actions they associate with the theme.

### What to do

➤ Select one action to begin working with.

➤ Begin by physically exploring as many different ways of doing the action. The action should not be embellished or decorated in any way but carefully observed and performed simply but precisely.

➤ Each person selects one way of doing the action that they want to work on more precisely.

➤ Reduce the action to no more, or less, than five movements.

➤ Ensure that each component of the action is clear and precise. At this point the actions should still be clearly recognisable.

At this point you are going to transform your action into, what Barba would call, an **ideogram**. The Chinese and Japanese language, in its written form, is made up of characters or ideograms. For example, the ideogram for China is made up of two signs, or two components, one meaning 'central' and the other 'land'.

Your five movements are like five components that, when put together, create a physical ideogram of the theme you are exploring.

You are now going to play with performing your ideogram in many different ways. Each time you try a different rhythm or dynamic, work on it slowly and carefully. Always seek to be as precise as possible before you move on to the next stage.

➤ Make each component of the ideogram as large as possible, Barba would say 'elaborate'.

➤ Reduce each component to as small a movement as possible, without losing any of the intensity of energy and precision.

➤ Apply different rhythms and pace to the actions: fast, slow, flowing, staccato.

➤ Recreate the ideogram with different parts of the body; for example, the nose, a knee, a finger, the eyes, a toe.

- Use different parts of the body as a platform for the movements. For example, you might use your thigh as a platform and your elbow will perform the movements on your thigh.
- Imagine that your arm is a paintbrush and paint the ideogram, in clean strokes, onto an imaginary canvas in front of you.
- Imagine that the canvas is several metres away from you, and then only a few centimetres away.
- Make the canvas huge, and then very small.
- Play with combining any of the ways that you have worked with so far.

As a sequence of actions the ideogram forms a very simple score. Each time you colour, or elaborate, the actions, the actions become less literal and more abstract. However, your internal score replays the original literal actions. To you there is a logic to your movements that is not obvious in the external, physical actions, or to a spectator. This is what Barba refers to in *The Paper Canoe* as the blood and skin of an exercise (1995: 155): the blood remains the same while the skin changes.

- Having worked on your ideogram on a vertical plane, work on it on the horizontal plane. Translate the actions into movements across space, using large steps, in slow motion, delicate steps, small tiptoeing steps.
- Return to some of the different ways of using your feet from Section 1 and try them with your ideogram.
- You might now try the sequence using, what Roberta Carreri calls, 'extrovert' and 'introvert' actions (see the work demonstration video *Traces in the Snow* (1994) and Carreri, 2000, which is the edited text of the demonstration in written form). As she explains, 'extrovert' can be understood as open actions, and 'introvert' as closed actions.
- Try the sequence with the hands extrovert but the chest introvert, or the pelvis extrovert but the feet introvert.
- Again, play with the many different possibilities of size, speed and different qualities of energy.

Having worked on numerous possibilities, compose your ideogram using what you consider to be the most interesting colours or 'elaborations'. Remember to use the principles that you have been developing in both

Section 1 and Section 2 of this chapter. Your sequence should last for about two minutes.

➤    Learn and fix the sequence.
➤    Without words, find a partner.
➤    Teach each other the sequence you have developed.
➤    With the two sequences you now have, work together to interweave the movements and create a dialogue between the two of you.

### What to note

None of the work here should be undertaken lightly, each section should be worked on thoroughly. The aim is to develop your creative capacity, your discipline, both mentally and physically, and your ability to transform your body away from its everyday mannerisms.

### Development

Having constructed a short physical score from an initial action, you are now going to develop an internal score of images that you associate with the physical score. The internal score, or story, need only make sense to you, and is a way of fixing the work and ensuring that you are creatively engaged, both physically and mentally.

The next section introduces you to two further ways of developing a montage. A montage is a term sometimes used by Odin, in a similar way to score; it is a sequence created and composed from a series of random images and associations that we each derive from a particular stimulus. A starting point for generating images comes from playing with an object, for example a piece of cloth, a wooden stick, or a fan. It is often better to work with something that either has no specific use, or is unfamiliar to your everyday behaviour.

➤    Begin by working with an object.
➤    Begin physically working in a space and exploring the size, weight, balance and resistance of the object.
➤    As you keep moving in the space, playing with the object, discover actions that you associate with a mental picture.

### What to note

It is important that you do not first imagine a picture and then recreate the action, but work with impulse, and so, through constant movement, discover the pictures. This is what Roberta Carreri calls 'thinking in movement' (see *Traces in the Snow*, 1994, and also Carreri, 2000: 60).

Once you have discovered 10 to 15 pictures or images then put them together to make a montage. The pictures may not have a relationship to each other at this point but once you have structured them into a montage you can then improvise the story that they tell to you. The logic of the story comes from your personal associations and may be more like the stories we conjure from our dreams.

### Additional developments

An exercise that might help here is to play a variation on 'word association'.

➤ In pairs, one of you begins by presenting a still image.
➤ A second person responds immediately by presenting a still image that responds through their association with the first image.
➤ And so on.

A development of this exercise entails each person writing down a list of eight words that they associate with a given first word or theme, for example, a theme might be 'leaving' and the chain of words might be: visitor, disruption, journey, storm, moon, reunited, gift, betrayal.

➤ Either in pairs, or as a whole group, make a list of eight words.
➤ Call out each word.
➤ Each individual will immediately make an image that they associate with the given word. The eight images form the basis of a score and can then be worked (coloured or elaborated) on further – look back over what you have done in the earlier sections of this workshop.

If you are working from a given theme, then your images may come from bits of stories you have read, pictures you have seen, songs you have sung, films you have seen. The richer your well of images, stories and associations, the richer your work will be. You do not need to explain your choice of image or association.

Try creating a montage of images from the theme 'Behind the Green Door'.

➤ Do not sit and think but move in the space, improvising your responses to the theme and create your own 'story'.
➤ Use the 'story' as the basis for creating a score.
➤ Transfer the actions of the 'story' to an object and through the object replay the 'story'.
➤ Play with changing levels and direction of movement.
➤ Discover further images from associations that come to you as you play with the 'story' in the space.

We have now explored three different ways of developing a montage:

1 Creating a movement score from an initial action, and creating our own story from our associations with the physical score.
2 Working with an object to create images and then a story.
3 Working from a given theme.

Each time you have started from a point of familiarity and then moved away from that point towards a more abstract way of creating a score. This is because you are trying to find the unexpected, the surprising and the most interesting work. Theatrically, the most straightforward path from A to B is usually the least interesting. Working in this way may appear overly complicated but it allows you to free up your creative potential.

### What to note

In each case your montage is personal and only you know the logic of the associations. Once you have learnt and fixed the score you can then begin to play with the size, speed and dynamic of each part of it. What is important here is that although the outside skin may change, the inside story can always stay the same (the blood and the skin image used by Barba). The actions all have a quality of presence that is vital to performance and this is because each movement is informed by the associations and stories that you have created. You can continue to elaborate the montage material by working with another performer who has created his or her own montage. As you did with the ideogram exercise, you can look for ways of interweaving the two montage sequences to create a physical dialogue. Neither performer needs to know what the other performer's hidden story or subscore is to create the dialogue.

The approach to developing a physical score and subscore is replicated when you create the vocal score and subscore. You may be given a theme and then find a piece of text that you associate with the theme. It may be a poem, or a piece of prose. You might then find a song that you associate with the theme, and use the tune for the song when speaking a different piece of text. This is not for the sake of making the spoken score sound strange, but so that you might be surprised by what you find and begin to creatively explore the vocal possibilities of the score. You might take the physical movements from a score that have a subscore and reproduce the physical actions vocally as you speak the text. You might have a range of different associations that you can use with the spoken text and you should try working with all of them.

For example, 'Behind the Green Door' there may be a swarm of rats running around; we may use this image to inform our voice when we say the first part of the text and, in our subscore, we jump on a chair, but the chair wobbles, and we fall off. We then discover the rats are not interested in us but are very busy tidying up before they go on holiday.

All of these seemingly random thoughts make up your subscore and you express these visual images vocally through the intonation of the text. The text may, for example, be the narrative noted above, or it may be a completely different piece of text. Try the above example, first by using your own images and associations to create a story, then using your voice to express the actions as you tell the story. Finally, apply the vocal sequence as you tell a different story. It is a very demanding exercise because you have to do two different things at the same time. However, the exercise can create some fascinating and exciting material.

### Connections

When Barba asks actors to prepare work for him to see from a given theme, he will often ask them to prepare a 'proposition'. The 'proposition' will come in the form of montage material: their scores and subscores. Barba will see the material and, using the parts that he finds most interesting, he will begin to explore the work, often by placing it in a completely different context. For example, the physical score you have created in response to the theme 'Behind the Green Door' might now be used in a scene where you are required to announce to your people that they are at war. See if you can apply your physical score to this context. What do you need to alter? Can you keep the subscore the same?

The director's subscore need not be divulged to the actors, as the actor's subscore need not be revealed to either the other actors or the director. The director provides the themes for the actors to individually work on, and they present their scores as material for the director to work with.

## SECTION 4: APPLYING THE ODIN APPROACH TO A TEXT – WORKING WITH A PLAY TEXT

Both of the other accounts in this section come from workshops that have been especially created by Odin actors in response to the often-asked question: can the Odin approach to acting be applied to work with a theatre script? The scripted texts used in these two demonstrations are only worked on during the actual workshop demonstration presented as a part of an Odin Week. The actors have no intention of performing the whole play.

The workshops have been developed as an exercise by and for the actors, to explore how their approach to acting works in different contexts.

### Workshop 4.5: 'Text, action and relations in Shakespeare's play *Othello*'

The first account documents a workshop prepared and presented by Julia Varley and Tage Larsen. The workshop focuses on the scene between Othello and Iago from Act III, Scene 3 of Shakespeare's play *Othello*.

#### *What they did*

The two actors began the demonstration by first speaking the lines of the scene out loud, as neutrally as possible. They explained that, once they had learnt the lines, they had played a game of word association selecting key words from the scene. Alongside doing the 'word association' exercise, they looked at music that might be interesting to work with as another stimulus. They chose a traditional African song because the character of Othello is a foreigner in the play. The song came from the **Candomblé** tradition and represents the character of a warrior. Julia and Tage learnt both the song and the Candomblé dance for the warrior, and this became the opening sequence. Rather than studying the psychology of the scene, the two actors began work on physical actions, creating a physical dialogue of actions and reactions. These actions did not come from the *Othello* text, so it was not a literal translation of the words into actions; rather, the actions came from the two actors playing together. When they found actions or images in their play that they liked they named them, so as to remember them. Because the two actors are so familiar with working in this way their play is very rich; that is, the actions are varied in texture, dynamic and rhythm, etc. At this stage in the demonstration the actions and the sequences that they are building do not mean anything but are alive and believable. Through play, the two actors create a physical dialogue that they then work on individually, in order to create their own personal subscore. Once their individual scores of physical actions and subscores are fixed they then come back together and begin to find ways to build stronger ties between the two scores by 'colouring' the actions. For example, in the physical score, one of the actors had made the action of pushing a giant rock, while the other actor had made the action of welcoming a long lost friend. Within the context of the scene this second action may have some logic but the first action does not. By reducing the pushing action to merely holding the hands, palms outwards, in front of the body (keeping the same intensity of energy) the action works; this is what is meant by 'colouring'. This part of the process allows the actors to become more familiar with the elements that they have selected. They each have a sequence and can begin to play at making actions larger, smaller, slower, etc. An action with an arm may occasionally be changed and performed by another part of the body; an action done standing up may be done kneeling down. Many possibilities are tried in the process of 'colouring' before anything is fixed. Inevitably, the process of 'colouring' will mean that some of the actions will change but the core of the action will always remain. The text and actions have not been put together at this stage. Once the process of 'colouring' has been completed, and the actors have selected what they consider to be the most interesting ways of performing the actions, they will fix the score. They can now begin the sequence with the Candomblé song and dance and follow on with the physical score and the spoken text. Although the score has not been designed to work with the text, it is exciting and surprising, as an audience member watching the demonstration, to discover that there are many incidental meeting points between the different layers of the performance. The next phase of the work requires the two actors to return to exploring further ways in which the score may be inflected. As well as selecting and fixing what works, the actors need to identify where there are problems in the relationship between the different layers of performance and how the problems might be solved. It is only at this stage that the two actors choose to discuss the scene intellectually. Prior to this stage, the two actors had only wanted to work with association and impulse but, once that phase had produced a score, they researched the play historically and critically. They discussed their findings and what particular ideas and themes they wanted to emphasise in the playing of the scene.

At the stage in which the workshop was being presented, during the Odin Week in 2002, both actors had reverted to working separately to develop the physical elements, but this time in conjunction with their knowledge of the characters and the written text.

I could see that, as the process had been developed, the casual and playful choices that the actors initially made had now been refined, and the choices validated by their understanding of the play. What was fascinating to see demonstrated was the way in which they as actors could continue to adapt their actions to the meaning of the text, without losing the subscore. Tage and Julia had been working on the scene over many work demonstrations and were still being surprised at the connections they were finding. Discoveries were still being made because they were still questioning and working with the logic of the score and script.

At the end of the work demonstration, Tage and Julia spoke about where the work might go. The next stage of the process might involve developing the vocal score. This would initially come from the two actors proposing ideas of ways to colour the spoken text; for example, using the voice to follow the movements of a fly, while speaking the lines of the scene. Separating the words from the context of the scene, and trying different vocal patterns and rhythms, allows the actor to make discoveries in the text that they might not have found had they only been looking at the meaning of the words.

The aim of the work is to make the text clear, not affected or artificial; it is not about making strange movements and sounds for the sake of it but to justify the movements and make them natural. The process of refining the physical and vocal actions may appear to be a long process, but the material that emerges from the play of associations is surprising and exciting. Shakespeare's text is central in the work demonstration; this is not the case in the performance work that Odin makes, where there is no single text.

## Workshop 4.6: 'Dialogue between two actors'

The final example comes from a work demonstration presented by Torgeir Wethal and Roberta Carreri as part of an Odin Week. Again, the demonstration explores the relationship between their approach to acting and traditional theatre; in this instance they use the final scene in the play *A Doll's House* by Ibsen to serve their experiment. The scene is between Nora and Helmer and runs from where Nora tells Helmer she is leaving and freeing him completely, to the end of the play. They began work on the demonstration in 1998 and only work on it in front of the spectators attending an Odin Week. The approach they took was to explore the characters individually and find ways of bringing the characters to life. This is a radically different approach to working on a performance from that usually taken at Odin.

### What they did

Having read the text, they selected the final scene to work on. Torgeir began by looking at what performance materials he already had in his store of experience that might be useful in relation to the character of Helmer. He was interested in the idea that the play explored the life of a man and so he constructed a performance sequence that showed the life of a man and then reversed the playing of it. He then reflected on the sequence to see whether there were fragments, images, moments that might fit with the text.

Roberta's approach began with her finding associations with words in the text that could be translated into images. This is an approach she would use when working on an Odin performance, but the difference this time was that the associations were not her own but what she thought Nora's would be. The associations came from ideas in the text and included the lark, children, being strong and wedding vows. Along with the props that Roberta chose to work with from the beginning as part of her costume (a wedding ring, a handbag, a travelling bag and a set of keys), these images were translated into actions then put together to create a basic score that served as an entrance for Nora into Helmer's world. Meanwhile, Torgeir had found a poem that he thought might be useful, but having tried to work with the poem and produced no interesting material, he tore it up. He then followed the logic of this action and proceeded to burn the paper. Torgeir was intrigued by these actions and decided that they might make possible material for the performance.

Initially, Roberta found the action of the text was dominated by the dynamic of the physical actions from her score. She needed to work at reducing the physical score to a size that would be acceptable to the conventions of the **naturalistic** style required by the play. So a demonstrative action of strength towards Helmer was reduced and reduced to just a flicker of a finger. Other actions were reduced to a shift of weight or a glance downwards of the eyes; however, inside the actor, the action is still clear and gives the external performance a richness and decidedness. Other problems arose between the text and their personal scores that needed to be solved and these involved the use of space, the spoken text, props and furniture.

Once the two actors had prepared a score for a section they came together to create both a spoken as well as a physical dialogue. They observed and responded to each other's actions and rhythms, focusing on the actions. They next worked on the room that the scene takes place in, playing with the effects of changing the size and what was in the room. The different decisions concerning the room were then considered as they began to find ways of colouring the text. Keeping the score of actions, but changing the intensity and the size of the actions according to the size of the space the actors agreed to move in, they demonstrated how the text could be played with if coloured by the idea of it being a love scene, or coloured by the idea that they were afraid to wake the children or fencing with the words. It was clear from the demonstration that their approach to the text had opened up all kinds of possibilities, and surprise moments that revealed exciting possibilities in the relationship between Nora and Helmer. They were challenged by the process of applying their approach to acting to a text where the work had to serve the characters and the logic of the characters, and where the physical score had to emerge from the text. The process revealed restrictions and limitations on their usual creative approach but it did serve to illustrate how much could be creatively and interpretatively gained by actors, should they choose to work in this way. It is important to remember that if you go straight from A to B in your work you are not creating any room for discoveries or surprises to be made.

# GLOSSARY

**acculturation** 15

A consciously learnt technique of behaviour, for example, ballet or the acting techniques developed by Brecht and Barba. See Barba and Savarese, 1991: 190.

**anima** 60

A term used by Barba to denote a soft and delicate energy. See Barba, 1995: 61.

**animus** 60

A term used by Barba to denote a strong and vigorous energy. See Barba, 1995: 61.

**Artaud**, Antonin (1896–1948) 23

French actor and writer. Most well known for his theatre manifestos 'The Theatre of Cruelty' and 'Theatre and its Double'. He advocated a Total Theatre that embraced all the senses and challenged the perceptions of the audience.

**Barong** 80

A general term for a mask representing an animal. The best known is the Barong Ket that resembles a dragon-like lion. See Bandem and deBoer, 1995.

**Bausch**, Pina (1940–) 59

A German choreographer and dancer, her work continues to explore the idea of dance theatre.

**Beijing Opera** 13

Also referred to as Peking Opera. Established more than 200 years ago, this form of Chinese opera is characterised by its spectacular acrobatic performers, elaborate facial make-up, magnificent costumes and fairy tale stories.

**Brecht**, Bertolt (1898–1956) 23

German dramatist, director and poet. Most notably Brecht developed the concept of *Verfremdungseffekt*, a technique used by actors that translates as 'to make strange'. He developed one of the most influential theatre ensembles in Europe, the Berliner Ensemble, and has had a significant influence on European theatre practice.

**Buyo** 47

Japanese dance often used in relation to traditional **Kabuki** dance. See Ortolani, 1990.

**Candomblé** 144

A dance form associated with Brazil but more specifically with the celebration of the Orixa religion that originated in the Yoruba people from Africa. See **Orixa**.

**Chekhov**, Michael (1891–1955) 63

Russian actor and, most importantly, the author of *To the Actor* (1991 edition published under the title *On the Technique of Acting*), one of the most important and influential actor training manuals of the twentieth century. See Chamberlain in Hodge, 2000, for further information.

**commedia dell'arte** 14

An Italian form of comic and farcical improvisation dating back to the sixteenth century.

**communitas** 10

A term used by the anthropologist Victor **Turner** to discuss particular types of human interaction. Communitas is defined as an open, spontaneous relationship that is not impeded by constraints of social norms but is open to creative possibilities. Turner describes three different types, namely 'spontaneous', 'ideological' and 'normative'. Spontaneous communitas, the one most useful to theatre, describes a collective experience of understanding or a mutual emotional response that occurs between people totally absorbed in an event. See Turner, 1982: 47–51 for further definitions.

**concrete** 22

Defined by Barba as '*con*, together, and *crescere*, to grow, that is, to let oneself change' (Barba, 1995: 89).

**condensation** 87

A term coined by Freud in *The Interpretation of Dreams* (1900) to suggest the act of summarising or condensing.

**Copeau**, Jacques (1878–1949) 13

Worked in France as a theatre teacher and director. He believed in training actors in a range of skills from clowning to commedia.

**Craig**, Edward Gordon (1872–1966) 13

British theatre designer whose radical ideas have been very influential in the development of European theatre design. He is best known for his controversial ideas about the actor as *Uber-Marionette*.

**decided** 49

For the actor to be 'decided' means that thought and action are working together; a similar idea to being 'in the moment'.

**Decroux**, Etienne (1898–1991) 55

Reputed to be the founding father of modern mime.

**dilation** 37

To do with the excess of energy required by the performer when performing at an **extra-daily** level.

**displacement** 87

A term coined by Freud in *The Interpretation of Dreams* (1900) to describe the act of substituting one thing for another.

**Djimat**, I Made 12

Balinese performer and teacher who has contributed his performance expertise to **ISTA** sessions.

**dramaturgy** 10

A widely used term to denote the research work undertaken, both practical and scholarly, in preparation for a theatre production. See Barba, 1990, 2000b, and Christofferson, 1993, for further details of how Odin specifically use the term.

**Ego** 86

A part of the mind that governs and controls our perception and construction of reality. A term used by **Freud** in conjunction with, and also in conflict with, **Id**.

**Eisenstein**, Sergei (1898–1948) 59

Most well known as a Russian film director who, as a student, studied at **Meyerhold**'s experimental theatre studio and also directed theatre. Especially important was his experimental work with montage. He was interested in the effect of juxtaposing images that were not obviously linked to create new meanings.

**embodied** 31

A tangible or visible expression of an idea, quality or experience.

**energy** 3

Holds a central position in Barba's work on actor training. An actor must be able to harness, sustain, control and focus energy effectively in performance to attract and hold the attention of the spectator.

**equivalence** 22

In art, equivalence is not to imitate or reconstruct nature but to find another way of reproducing reality using displacement and counter-weight. See Barba and Savarese, 1991: 95–103 and Barba, 1995: 30–32.

**extra-daily** 9

Techniques, or particular ways of using the body, used by the performer 'which do not respect the habitual conditionings of the use of the body' (Barba, 1995: 15–16).

**Fo**, Dario (1926–) 12

Italian actor and playwright. Fo won the Nobel Prize for Literature in 1997. His work is characterised by political satire and farce.

**Freud**, Sigmund (1856–1939) 86

First to develop the term psychoanalysis, born in Moravia but settled in Vienna and later worked in London. He is most well known for his work on analysing dreams, the 'Freudian slip' and the effects of unconscious desires and repression.

**fuzzy narrative** 96

A term derived from fuzzy logic that I am using to denote a network of narrative strands within the performance, which are brought into focus by the creative reading of the spectator. Fuzzy logic is a term applied to computer programs developing artificial intelligence. These programs aim to mimic 'the way that humans learn within a context of real world fuzziness: humans do not act in accordance with formal rules so much as by approximation and adjustment' (Sim, 2001: 252).

**Gambuh** 78

The oldest surviving form of dance drama in Bali. See Bandem and deBoer, 1995.

**Gamelan** 93

A term used to describe all types of Balinese orchestra made up of percussive instruments. See Bandem and deBoer, 1995.

**Garuda** 77

A mythical bird found in Thai mythology and Hinduism.

**Goethe**, Johann Wolfgang von (1749–1832) 76

German poet, novelist and dramatist.

**Grotowski**, Jerzy (1933–1999) 4

A director who, working in Poland, founded The Theatre of Thirteen Rows that later became the Theatre Laboratory. He was specifically interested in the development of the actor's creative energy. His work continues at the Pontedera centre in Italy.

**Id** 99

A Freudian term for the unconscious part of the mind that seeks out pleasure.

**ideogram** 138

Barba gives an explanation and example of what he means by ideogram in *The Paper Canoe* (pages 30–32). In order to reach a point where we can perform a complex concept we need to begin with **concrete** actions. The composition of the concrete actions can then be refined and refined to communicate, in abstract form, many possible meanings and ideas.

**improvisation** 19

As Barba argues, this can mean many different things but he sees it as 'thought/action on the riverbed of a physical score' (Barba, 1995: 72 plus note 30).

**inculturation** 14

Socially learnt behaviour. 'The process of passive sensory-motor absorption of the daily behaviour of a given culture' (Barba and Savarese, 1991: 189).

**intercultural** 85

In theatrical terms, can mean the mixing of different performance traditions to create a hybrid form. See Pavis, 1996a.

**intertextual** 98

A complex critical term that can be applied and understood in many ways. See Allen, 2000. On one level it can be understood as the quotation of, or references to, other texts to create a new text or to open up meanings in a text.

**ISTA** 1

The International School of Theatre Anthropology. See Hastrup, 1996, for details.

*jo-ha-kyu* 61

Arguably the most important aesthetic concept in **Noh**. *Jo* means beginning or preparation, *ha* means breaking and *kyu* means rapid or urgent. See Komparu, 1983, and Barba, 1995: 69.

**Kabuki** 13

Traditional form of Japanese popular theatre which began towards the end of the sixteenth century. See Ortolani, 1990.

**Kathakali** 6

A traditional form of dance drama from Kerala in south-west India. See Zarrilli, 2000.

**keras** 114

Balinese term for strong and vigorous energy. See Bandem and deBoer, 1995.

**kinaesthetic** 96

Also referred to as muscle sense. Explores the ways in which we perceive motion or weight in our muscles.

**Koestler**, Arthur (1905–1983) 62

Hungarian born, British novelist.

**Laban**, Rudolf von (1879–1958) 67

Hungarian dancer, choreographer and theorist whose particular research was in close analysis of human movement. He is most well known for developing a system of dance notation.

**Lecoq**, Jacques (1921–1999) 12

Founder of the International Theatre School of Jacques Lecoq in Paris. Lecoq was a mime artist, theatre director and teacher. His school teaches movement, mime, bouffons and clowning.

**Legong** 47

A classical female dance drama form, usually performed by two or three young girls. See Bandem and deBoer, 1995.

**leitmotiv** 85

A musical theme which illustrates or depicts a certain character, idea or situation in a drama.

**liminal** 106

A term used by Victor **Turner** in relation to ritual and perform-ance to describe the space in which both ritual and performance take place, that is 'betwixt and between' one space and another. See Schechner, 1985, and Turner, 1982.

**Madame Butterfly** 104

An opera by the Italian composer Puccini, adapted from a story by John Luther Long. The story tells of a young Japanese girl who is ruthlessly seduced and then abandoned by an American naval officer. She bears his child and waits for him to return. Finally, giving up hope, she commits suicide.

**manis** 114

> Balinese term for soft, sweet and refined energy. See Bandem and deBoer, 1995.

**Marlowe**, Christopher (1564–1597) 76

> English poet and playwright.

**Meyerhold**, Vsevolod (1874–1940) 5

> Russian actor and director who worked alongside **Stanislavsky** and ran the Moscow Arts Studio. Worked against naturalism in acting and founded a system of training called bio-mechanics.

**modernist** 25

> A movement in the arts, in the West, that began towards the end of the nineteenth century and affected much of the twentieth century. It is defined by a call to 'make it new'.

**montage** 18

> see **scenic montage**

**naturalistic** 148

> In drama it denotes a period, from the late nineteenth and into the early twentieth centuries, of European plays sharing similar concerns, for example, human agency and environmental influence. The term is most associated with the plays of **Chekhov** and Ibsen, and is often understood in relation to theatre that depicts a life-like representation of the world.

**Noh** 22

> A Japanese genre of dance theatre developed during the fourteenth century and one of the most important forms of theatre to the present day.

**Odin Week** 24

> A week of work and performances run by members of the Odin Teatret for a group of participants from around the world. Odin Weeks are held most years at the theatre in Holstebro.

**Odissi** 65

> A classical dance form from east India that originates in the temple dances of Orissa. The form performed today has been reconstructed and popularised once more by the dancer Sanjukta

**Panigrahi**, who co-founded **ISTA** with Barba. The form is typified by the *mudras* (hand gestures that have specific meanings) and the *Tribhangi* (a concept that divides the body into three parts) that creates characteristic poses. See Barba and Savarese, 1991.

**onnagata** 78

In **Kabuki**, a male performer of female roles. See Ortolani, 1990.

**Orixa** 87

Understood to be archetypal energies that are like Saints. There are hundreds of different Orixa and the main ones are represented through the **Candomblé** dance.

**Pangpang** 77

**Rangda**'s assistant in the dance drama *Calonarang*. See Bandem and deBoer, 1995.

**Panigrahi**, Sanjukta (1945–1997) 12

As an Indian dancer, choreographer and teacher, Sanjukta was most importantly known for her revival of the classical Indian dance **Odissi**. Sanjukta was an internationally respected dancer who also worked closely with Eugenio Barba on the **ISTA** project.

**peripeteia** 63

A term from Aristotle's structure of tragedy, 'an interweaving of events which causes an action to develop in an unforeseeable way, or causes it to conclude in a way opposite to how it began' (Barba, 1995: 89).

**pre-condition** 62

Used in conjunction with creative, as in creative pre-condition, and derived from **Koestler**'s definition of a creative act as: 'accomplished through a preliminary regression to a more primitive level . . . a process of negation and disintegration which prepares the leap towards the result' (Barba, 1995: 87).

**pre-expressive** 22

A term used by Barba to describe the recurring principles underlying the work of the performer in relation to energy and organisation. See Barba, 1995.

**presence** 3

*see* **scenic presence**

**proxemics** 96

The study and interpretation of spatial relationships between individuals in social interaction.

**Rangda** 77

Known as 'the widow' mask in Bali. Usually a demonic character who appears in many dance dramas. See Bandem and deBoer, 1995.

**Rembrandt**, Harmenszoon van Rijn (1606–1669) 20

Dutch painter, draftsman and etcher.

**sats** 26

A Norwegian word translated by the words 'impulse', 'preparation', 'to be ready to . . .' – the instant that precedes the action. See Barba, 1995: 40.

**scenic bios** 49

*see* **scenic presence**

**scenic montage** 18–19

The composition of scenes. See Watson, 1993: 102.

**scenic presence** 27

This and 'scenic behaviour' are a result of **scenic bios**. These terms are used by Barba to discuss the performer's ability to use energy and the body at an extra-daily level to attract the attention of the spectator. Scenic presence, or behaviour, is the result, the particular performance technique and style used by a performer. Scenic bios denotes the underlying principles that Barba argues are shared by all performers whatever particular tradition they come from and these form the principles of the **pre-expressive**.

**Schechner**, Richard (1934–) 9

American theatre director and academic, who has written extensively about theatre and performance. Schechner pioneered work in the field of Performance Studies.

**score** 19

A term used by Odin to denote both the visible and invisible (**sub-score**) performance material that the actors and director construct for a theatre production and/or workshop demonstration.

**semiotics** 87

Broadly, the study of signs. For specific information regarding Theatre Semiotics, see Aston and Savona, 1991; Elam, 1988; and Pavis, 1982.

**Shishi** 80

A mythical lion figure in Japan.

**signified** 93

The mental idea that the **signifier** relates to.

**signifier** 93

A sound (for example, a word spoken), a mark on a page (a word in its written form) or image (for example, a photograph) that we associate with, represents and/or stands in for something.

**socialist** 3

A supporter of a political theory or system known as socialism. Socialism argues that people should all have an equal say and equal power to control the means of production. Socialism argued for an end to private property.

**Stanislavsky**, Konstantin (1863–1938) 5

Russian actor, director and teacher who founded the Moscow Art Theatre with Vladimir Nemirovich-Danchenko in 1898. Developed a system for training actors that is still a major influence on the training of actors in Europe.

**subscore** 32

An internal score constructed by the performer that has a personal logic based on associations and images drawn from the given theme of the production.

**Third Theatre** 16

A term coined by Barba to describe theatre that is neither commercially driven nor experimental but independent and defined by those performers and makers who are, frequently, not traditionally trained but driven by experience to make the theatre that they consider to be important. See Barba, 1986a, and Watson *et al.*, 2002.

**Topeng** 77

A masked dance drama from Bali. See Bandem and deBoer, 1995.

**transculturally** 97

Used here to describe a theatre that is not rooted in any one cultural tradition.

**Turner**, Victor (1920–1983) 9

Born in Scotland, Turner was an anthropologist who lived and worked in America. He is most renowned for his important and extensive work in the field of ritual and performance.

**UNESCO** 3

Abbreviation for United Nations Educational, Scientific, and Cultural Organisation.

**Vietnam War** (1965–1973) 7

A war where the US intervened and fought on behalf of the South Vietnamese in their battle with the communist-backed North Vietnamese.

**Wilson**, Robert (1941–) 34

A highly acclaimed American theatre director and artist. See Drain, 1995, and Huxley and Witts, 1996, for further information.

# BIBLIOGRAPHY

Andreasen, John and Kuhlmann, Annelis (eds) (2000) *Odin Teatret 2000*, Acta Jutlandica: Aarhus University Press.

Allen, Graham (2000) *Intertextuality*, London: Routledge.

Aston, Elaine and Savona, George (1991) *Theatre as Sign System: A Semiotics of Text and Performance*, London: Routledge.

Bandem, I Made and deBoer, Fredrik Eugene (1995) *Balinese Dance in Transition: Kaja and Kelod*, 2nd edition, Oxford: Oxford University Press.

Barba, Eugenio (1965) *Alla Ricerca del Teatro Perduta*, translated as *In Search of Theatre*, Padova: Marsillo Editore.

—— (1979) *The Floating Islands*, Holstebro: Drama.

—— (1982) 'Theatre Anthropology', *Tulane Drama Review* 26(2) (T36): 5–32.

—— (1985) 'The Dilated Body: On the Energies of Acting', *New Theatre Quarterly*, 1(4), November: 369–382.

—— (1986a) *Beyond the Floating Islands*, New York: PAJ.

—— (1986b) 'ISTA: Between the Face and the Mask', in *Village Voice*, 25 November: 96 and 98.

—— (1987) 'The Actor's Energy: Male/Female versus Animus/Anima', *New Theatre Quarterly* 3(11): 237–240.

—— (1988a) 'The Way of Refusal: The Theatre's Body in Life', *New Theatre Quarterly* 4(16): 291–299.

—— (1988b) 'About the Visible and the Invisible in the Theatre and About ISTA in Particular', *Tulane Drama Review* 32(3) (T119), Fall: 7–14.

—— (1988c) 'Eurasian Theatre', *Tulane Drama Review* 32(3) (T119): 126–130.

—— (1990) 'Four Spectators', *Tulane Drama Review* 34(1) (T125): 96–100.

—— (1991) 'The Third Theatre. A Legacy from Us to Ourselves', *New Theatre Quarterly* 8(29): 3–9.

—— (1995) *The Paper Canoe: A Guide to Theatre Anthropology*, London: Routledge.

—— (1997) 'An Amulet made of Memory. The Significance of Exercises in the Actor's Dramaturgy', *Tulane Drama Review* 41(4) (T156), Winter: 127–132.

—— (1999a) *Land of Ashes and Diamonds*, Aberystwyth: Black Mountain Press.

—— (1999b) *Theatre: Solitude, Craft, Revolt*, Aberystwyth: Black Mountain Press.

—— (1999c) 'My Grandfather Konstantin Sergeyevich: An Interview with Eugenio Barba', *Mime Journal* edition 'Transmission', Winter: 28–51.

—— (2000a) 'Tacit Knowledge: Heritage and Waste', *New Theatre Quarterly*, 16(3) (NTQ 63), August: 263–276.

—— (2000b) 'The Deep Order Called Turbulence', *Tulane Drama Review* 44(4) (T168), Winter: 56–66.

—— and Savarese, Nicola (1991) *A Dictionary of Theatre Anthropology: The Secret Art of the Performer*, London: Routledge.

Calvino, Italo (1997) *Invisible Cities*, London: Vintage.

Carreri, Roberta (2000) 'Traces in the Snow', in John Andreasen and Annelis Kuhlmann (eds) *Odin Teatret 2000*, Acta Jutlandica: Aarhus University Press.

Chamberlain, Franc (2000) 'Theatre Anthropology: Definitions and Doubts', in Anthony Frost (ed.) *Theatre Theories from Plato to Virtual Reality*, Norwich: Pen and Inc.

Chekhov, Michael (2002 [1953]) *To the Actor*, London: Routledge.

Christofferson, Erik Exe (1993) *The Actor's Way*, London: Routledge.

De Marinis, Marco (1995) 'From Pre-Expressivity to the Dramaturgy of the Performer: An Essay on *The Paper Canoe*', in *Mime Journal* edition 'Incorporated Knowledge': 114–156.

Drain, Richard (ed.) (1995) *Twentieth Century Theatre: A Sourcebook*, London: Routledge.

Elam, Keir (1988) *The Semiotics of Theatre and Drama*, London: Routledge.

Freud, Sigmund (1991 [1900]) *The Interpretation of Dreams*, trans. James Strachey, Harmondsworth: Penguin.

Goethe, Johann Wolfgang von (1959) *Faust: A Tragedy – Parts One and Two*, trans. Philip Wayne, Harmondsworth: Penguin.

—— (2001) *Faust: A Tragedy: Interpretive Notes, Contexts, Modern Criticism*, trans. Walter Arndt, A Norton Critical Edition, London: Norton and Company.

Grotowski, Jerzy (1964) 'Dr. Faustus: Textual Montage', *Tulane Drama Review* 8(4) (T24), Summer: 120–133.

—— (1969) *Towards a Poor Theatre*, edited by Eugenio Barba, London: Methuen.

Hastrup, Kirsten (ed.) (1996) 'The Making of Theatre History', in *The Performer's Village*, Holstebro: Drama.

Hodge, Alison (ed.) (2000) *Twentieth Century Actor Training*, London: Routledge.

Huxley, Michael and Witts, Noel (eds) (1996) *The Twentieth Century Performance Reader*, London: Routledge.

Ibsen, Henrik (1993 [1879]) *A Doll's House*, London: J.M. Dent.

Jung, Carl (1972) *Two Essays on Analytical Psychology*, Princeton, NJ: Princeton University Press (translated from *Uber die Psychologie des Unbewussten*, Zurich: 1943, and *Die Beziehungenzwischen dem Ich und dem Unbewussten*, Zurich: 1928).

Kleist, Heinrich von ([1810]) 'On the Marionette Theatre', trans. Idris Parry for *Southern Cross Review*. Available at: www.southerncross review/9/kleist.htm

Koestler, Arthur (1959) *The Sleepwalkers*, New York: Macmillan.

Komparu, Kunio (1983) *The Noh Theatre: Principles and Perspectives*, New York: Weatherhill/Tankosha.

Marlowe, Christopher (1996) *Dr. Faustus*, London: Nick Hearn Books.

Munk, Erika (1986) 'Roles and Poles Apart', in *Village Voice*, 11 November: 89–90.

Odin Week (2001) Spoken quotations taken from the proceedings of this week.

Ortolani, Benito (1990) *The Japanese Theatre: From Shamanistic Ritual to Contemporary Pluralism*, revised edition, Princeton, NJ: Princeton University Press.

Pavis, Patrice (1982) *Languages of the Stage*, New York: PAJ.

—— (1992) *First Statement Regarding 'Underscoring'*, ISTA.

—— (1996a) *The Intercultural Reader*, London: Routledge.

—— (1996b) 'A Canoe Adrift', unpublished review.

—— (2003) *Analyzing Performance*, Ann Arbor, MI: Michigan University Press.

Schechner, Richard (1985) *Between Theatre and Anthropology*, Philadelphia, PA: University of Pennsylvania Press.

Shakespeare, William (1997) *Othello*, edited by E.A.J. Honigmann, Walton-on-Thames: Nelson (the Arden edition. Third series).

Sim, S. (ed.) (2001) *The Routledge Companion to Postmodernism*, London: Routledge.

Turner, Victor (1974) *Dramas, Fields, and Metaphors: Symbolic Action in Human Society*, Ithaca, NY: Cornell University Press.

—— (1982) *From Ritual to Theatre: The Human Seriousness of Play*, New York: PAJ Publications.

—— (1986) 'Dewey, Dilthey, and Drama: An Essay in the Anthropology of Experience', in Victor Turner and Edward Bruner (eds) *The Anthropology of Experience*, Urbana and Chicago, IL: University of Illinois Press.

Watson, Ian (1993) *Towards a Third Theatre*, London: Routledge.

—— *et al.* (2002) *Negotiating Cultures: Eugenio Barba and the Intercultural Debate*, Manchester: Manchester University Press.

Wright, Elizabeth (1984) *Psychoanalytic Criticism: Theory and Practice*, London: Routledge.

Zarrilli, Phillip (1988) 'For Whom Is the "Invisible" Not Visible', *Tulane Drama Review* 32(1) (T117), Spring: 95–106.

—— (2000) *Kathakali Dance Drama: Where Gods Come to Play*, London: Routledge.

## VIDEO LIST

*Physical Training at Odin Teatret* (1972) Directed by Torgeir Wethal. Produced by Odin Teatret Film.

*Vocal Training at Odin Teatret* (1972) Directed by Torgeir Wethal. Produced by Odin Teatret Film.

*The Million* (1979) Directed by Torgeir Wethal. Produced by Odin Teatret Film.

*The Gospel According to Oxyrhincus* (1991) Directed by Torgeir Wethal. Produced by Odin Teatret Film.

*The Dead Brother* (1993) Produced by Claudio Coloberti for Odin Teatret Film.

*The Echo of Silence* (1993) Produced by Claudio Coloberti for Odin Teatret Film.

*Traces in the Snow* (1994) Directed by Torgeir Wethal. Co-produced between Document Films, Athens, and Odin Teatret Film.

*Whispering Winds* (1997) Produced by Claudio Coloberti for Odin Teatret Film.

*Kaosmos* (1998) Directed by Peter Sykes. Co-produced between Peter Sykes Associates, Statens Filmcentral and Odin Teatret Film.

*Ego Faust* (2001) Directed by Luigi Rossini. Produced by Cometa Film for Odin Teatret Film.

*Doña Musica's Butterflies* (2002) Produced by Lars Arnfred film/Jan Rüsz.

# INDEX

Numbers in **bold** type indicate pages containing illustrations.